Advance Praise for Ecce Homo

Sam Balentine is arguably the most important ⸺ ⸺ ⸺theolog-ical interpreter of Scripture in his generation. Characteristically (as here) he combines his truth-telling passion and his cunning erudition. In this study he is concerned with pain and our capacity to see it well and faithfully in others: "Grief is the tax we pay for our attachments." His study pivots on the odd narrative of Jesus and his invitation to us to see him. In his expo-sition of his theme Balentine reaches widely into classical art, the Book of Job, and contemporary social reality. The outcome is a breathtaking presen-tation that will shift for the reader a perspective for seeing and embracing pain that is all around us. We may be deeply grateful to the well-beloved Sam for this daring book.

—Walter Brueggemann
Columbia Theological Seminary

Balentine takes on a subject that causes discomfort or pain to every Chris-tian, but no one talks about directly: How do we look upon the pain of *others* in a way that is a genuine and compassionate witness to our own faith? Beautifully yet simply written, keenly sensitive to Scripture, art, and instances of suffering in our own world and the lives around us, this is a book to be shared widely in the church and even beyond it.

—Ellen F. Davis
Amos Ragan Kearns Distinguished Professor
of Bible and Practical Theology
Duke University Divinity School

Ecce Homo, written by an accomplished biblical scholar well-versed in art historical method, offers insightful reflections on scriptural narratives and corresponding works of art. Samuel Balentine places each story in its original historical context while providing a relatable meaning for the contemporary reader. The art, selected from across the centuries, further allows the reader to "see" the biblical verse as Balentine guides us with his words along a journey originally presented as a Lenten preparation.

—Heidi J. Hornik
Professor of Art History and Interim Department Chair
Baylor University

Sam Balentine's Lenten reflections, *Ecce Homo*, invite us into profound contemplation of the One at the center of the Gospel passion narratives.

I love this book not only because it dramatically places us within the Gospel stories from multiple points of view from inside the text and outside and asks us to "Behold the Man" and because it so appealingly draws from the history of western art to illuminate the text like a shifting kaleidoscope, but also and primarily I love it because its invitation to behold Jesus brings before our sight our own sufferings and the sufferings of others. To see this way is to be transformed. Balentine does this with deep research and clear and compelling writing. We need this book now in our tragically broken world, for in "beholding the man" we can find hope.

—Kathleen M. O'Connor
William Marcellus McPheeters Professor
of Old Testament, Emerita
Columbia Theological Seminary Decatur, GA

Sam Balentine immerses readers in the story of Jesus' passion through a masterful reading of the Gospels, intertwined with interpretative history and art. His keen eye and hermeneutical skills call us to be more than detached onlookers. Balentine asks us to see, to feel, and to take our place in the Lenten journey.

—Kandy Queen-Sutherland
Sam R Marks Professor of Religious Studies
Stetson University

I have a confession to make: I often believe Old Testament scholars read the New Testament differently and (dare I say it?) *better* than many others, including—at least occasionally—New Testament experts. Some may think that opinion a sin that needs pardon, not just confession, but in this volume readers can judge for themselves as they watch renowned Old Testament theologian Samuel Balentine reflect on the texts and images that accompany the Lenten season. Lent is traditionally a time of sorrow and deprivation, but this book by one of our best interpreters is an occasion for joy and thankfulness. What a gift!

—Brent A. Strawn
Professor of Old Testament and Professor of Law
Duke University

ECCE HOMO
BEHOLD THE MAN

Smyth & Helwys Publishing, Inc.
6316 Peake Road
Macon, Georgia 31210-3960
1-800-747-3016

Library of Congress Cataloging-in-Publication Data

Names: Balentine, Samuel E. (Samuel Eugene), 1950- author.
Title: Ecce homo : behold the man : ethical imperatives of the Lenten
    journey / by Samuel E. Balentine.
Description: Macon, GA : Smyth & Helwys, 2020. | Includes bibliographical
    references.
Identifiers: LCCN 2020037648 (print) | LCCN 2020037649 (ebook) | ISBN
    9781641732642 (paperback) | ISBN 9781641732697 (ebook)
Subjects: LCSH: Lent.
Classification: LCC BV85 .B324 2020 (print) | LCC BV85 (ebook) | DDC
    242/.34--dc23
LC record available at https://lccn.loc.gov/2020037648
LC ebook record available at https://lccn.loc.gov/2020037649

Samuel E. Balentine

Ecce Homo
BEHOLD THE MAN

*Ethical Imperatives
of the
Lenten Journey*

Also by Samuel E. Balentine

The Hidden God:
The Hiding of the Face of God in the Old Testament

Prayer in the Hebrew Bible: The Drama of Divine-Human Dialogue

The Torah's Vision of Worship

Leviticus

Job
(Smyth & Helwys Bible Commentary)

Have You Considered My Servant Job?:
Understanding the Biblical Archetype of Patience

Wisdom Literature

"Look at Me and Be Appalled": Essays on Job, Theology, and Ethics

The Lure of Transcendence and the Audacity of Prayer:
Essays on Prayer in the Hebrew Bible

For Carson, David, Mark, and Doug

Contents

Preface

These presentations were originally delivered some years ago in the Westminster Canterbury Lenten Lecture Series in Richmond, Virginia. I am grateful to Dr. Ray Inscoe, Director of Pastoral Care, for the invitation and to the Westminster Canterbury community for supporting the series with faithful attendance and energizing discussion. The lectures were given over a five-week period, beginning the first week of Lent and concluding the week before Palm Sunday. I and my audience were embarking on a Lenten journey, following a path that begins with Pilate's charge to the crowd—"Behold the Man"—and ends with Christ's summons to his disciples—"Look at my hands and feet . . . . Touch me and see." What does Lent invite us to *see*—about God, about the world in which we live, about ourselves—that we had not seen clearly enough before we began this journey? What are we charged to *touch and feel*? What must we *do*, how must not only our words but also our deeds be different, if Easter rituals are to be anything more than sacramental babble?

I did not write the lectures to be published, hence their informal style and their hortatory tenor. Nonetheless, when I reread them during this last Lenten season, I thought they might be worthy of public distribution. I have added a few footnotes, cleaned up grammatical infelicities, and modified some (not all) of the time-specific illustrations, but otherwise I have resisted the temptation to revise them.

It is fitting and very satisfying that the lectures be published by Smyth & Helwys, with whom I have worked in a variety of capacities for many years. I am especially grateful to Keith Gammons for his enthusiastic support of this project and to his colleague Leslie Andres for her invaluable help with the visuals.

Finally, I dedicate this book to four dear friends who have journeyed with me over many years through thick and thin. To Carson Brisson, whose wit and wisdom continues to sustain me; to David Howell, who came to my rescue years ago when I most needed a friend and never left; to Mark Biddle, whose steadfast compassion has upheld me; and to Doug Peters, whose presence I have always felt even when we were apart, I say, "Thank you." Without each of you, I would be lost.

May 2020

Abbreviations

ABD	*Anchor Bible Dictionary*. Edited by David Noel Freeman. 6 vols. New York: Doubleday, 1992.
Ant.	Jewish Antiquities
Apol.	*Apologeticus*
AV	Authorized Version
CEB	Common English Bible
Embassy	*On the Embassy to Gaius*
Hist. eccl.	*Historia ecclesiastica*
J.W.	*Jewish War*
KJV	King James Version
NAB	New American Bible
NIB	*New Interpreter's Bible*. Edited by Leander E. Keck. 12 vols. Nashville: Abingdon, 1994–2004.
NIV	New International Version
NRSV	New Revised Standard Version
REB	Revised English Bible
Sanh.	Sanhedrin

Ecce Homo:
"Behold the Man"

The Lenten journey is mapped by an imperative, twice spoken, from different perspectives. The first perspective is that of Pilate, who presents Jesus—bound, scourged, crowned with thorns, and wearing a purple robe—with the words, "Behold the man" (Latin: *Ecce homo*; John 19:5). The second is that of the resurrected Christ who says to the disciples, "Look at my hands and feet; see that it is I myself. Touch me and see; for a ghost does not have flesh and bones as you see that I have" (Luke 24:39).

Pilate offers the perspective of the onlooker, one whose power and privilege make it possible to endorse the abuse of another person and to look on their suffering from a safe distance. Christ's words, on the other hand, convey the experience of one whose firsthand experience with suffering makes it impossible to patronize the reality of brokenness and loss. The Lenten journey requires that we understand what it means for people of faith to view suffering from both perspectives. How are we to respond to the two summonses from Pilate and Jesus? If we place ourselves in the crowd to whom Pilate presents Jesus, what are we supposed to see and know when we behold this beaten and condemned innocent man? If we locate ourselves among the disciples, what are we supposed to *see* when Jesus shows us his wounds and says, "Look at my hands and feet"? What are we supposed to see and *feel* when Jesus says, "Touch me and see"? How we answer these questions will define in large measure both the journey we are making toward the empty tomb and the affirmations we will speak as our own on Easter morning.

I. THE HOUR HAS COME: JOHN 18:28–19:16A

The Gospel of John's portrayal of Jesus is different from the accounts in Matthew, Mark, and Luke. Whereas the Synoptics begin the story with the birth of Jesus into the specific time and setting of first-century Palestine, John's Prologue begins with a much broader view. His first words announce a cosmic focus. He tells us from the outset that this story has meaning that cannot be limited to any specific time on the calendar or to any one place in history. In short, the Word made flesh has to do with the whole world, a world peopled with Pilates and disciples, with interested and disinterested onlookers, with believers both courageous and cowardly. In essence, John invites everyone, whatever his or her status in life may be, to "behold the man."

> In the beginning was the Word, and the Word was with God, and the Word was God. He was in the beginning with God. All things came into being through him, and without him not one thing came into being. What has come into being in him was life, and the life was the light of all people. The light shines in the darkness, and the darkness did not overcome it. (John 1:1-5)

John will narrow his focus in the subsequent verses to the witness of specific people in identifiable times and places, beginning with John the Baptist and then the Jews and the Gentiles who were contemporaries with this Jesus, but first he insists that this story has cosmic, transtemporal dimensions that extend much farther. Just how much farther can only be measured by the opening words, "In the beginning," which echo the pregnant report in Gen 1:1 that births our faith perspective on God's creation of the world. "In the beginning," John announces, there was God and there was the Word. From this beginning, there came life, not in the abstract but instead in the palpable, enfleshed body-and-mind form of human beings. Such life expresses itself as "light"; in the Word that embodies its fullest form—the Word made flesh in Jesus—this light is full of "grace and truth" (1:14) that beckons everything that has breath to set its compass to God's hopes and expectations for a fullness of life that exceeds anything else available in all of creation.

At the tail end of John's Prologue, however, there is a promise that portends precariousness. There is "light" in the world into which this Word comes, but there is also "darkness." The Prologue neither explains nor defines this darkness; it only puts us on notice that light is constantly interacting with it. If we take our cue from Genesis 1, then John may be alluding to the primordial darkness, which by God's design provides for the rhythmic and harmonious sequencing of day and night that structures life on this planet. But if so, then Genesis and John may also be preparing us to understand that even from the beginning darkness has the potential to be disruptive, to break out of its assigned place and wreak havoc on the world. The Genesis story of creation leads to the accounts of Adam and Eve's transgressions, Cain's murder of Abel, and the floodwaters that destroy Noah's world. Perhaps it is against this background of darkness's ever-present threat to light that we are meant to read John's words, "The light shines in the darkness, and the darkness did not overcome it" (v. 5).

Although these words tilt toward the positive, their affirmation seems fraught with the same tension that underlies Genesis 1. The tension in John's Prologue is conveyed by the shifting tenses used for the verbs. The light "shines" and continues to shine (*phainei*, present tense) in the world, affirming that in the end light governs darkness. The activity of the darkness is described in the past tense (*katalambanō*), which seems at first glance to affirm the same thing, and yet translations grapple with the meaning in different ways. NRSV's "and the darkness *did not* overcome it" and REB's "and the darkness *never mastered* it" both suggest a struggle with darkness that has already ended with light's victory (cf. NAB, CEB). NIV's "but the darkness *has not understood* it" (cf. KJV) suggests that even as the light *continues to shine*, the darkness *continues to display* an inability to recognize and understand what the light offers. Even if light's ultimate victory is assured, its competition for comprehension is not a struggle that can be confined to the past.

When John shifts focus from the primordial and eternal light (vv. 1-5) to the Word made body and flesh in the real world of time and space (vv. 10-13), he seems to have one eye turned to the abiding and endlessly human struggle to understand and embrace the light that the sad stories of Genesis 3–11 record.

> He [the Light] was in the world, and the world came into being through him; yet the world did not know him. He came to what was his own, and his own people did not accept him. But to all who received him, who believed in his name, he gave power to become children of God . . . . (vv. 10-12)

The ultimate victory of light over darkness may be defined as past tense, completed action, but the struggle of those who must decide for or against the light remains a present-tense conundrum. Some people accept the light; some do not. A New Testament scholar makes the point as follows: "As the Gospel [of John] unfolds, whether people believe in Jesus will hinge on what they are able to *know and see.*"[1]

From John's mesmerizing Prologue, with all of its promise and peril, which introduces the first half of his account of Jesus' story (John 1–12), we fast-forward to the second half of his Gospel. The transition from beginnings to endings is marked in 13:1, which reports that as the time to celebrate the Passover approached, Jesus knew that the hour was coming when those who had seen the light would have to make their decision. Either they would know and see and embrace the "grace and truth" that shined in their midst, or they would not. The "hour of decision" ticks past Jesus' last meal with the disciples, when he washed their feet in preparation for the journey that awaited them (13:1-38), then his farewell sermon and prayer, which voices his hope that they will stay the course, come what will (chs. 14–17). When the minute hand of the clock reaches the time of Jesus' arrest, trial, and death (18–19), John announces that the hour "has come" (16:32). For my purposes here, I invite you to ponder the possibility that when Pilate utters the words "Behold the man" (19:5), the time for all of us to decide what the Lenten journey means in real life has come.

---

1. G. O'Day, "The Gospel of John," *NIB*, vol. 9 (Nashville: Abingdon, 1995), 521 (emphasis added).

The seven scenes that comprise John's perspective on Jesus' trial track the outside-inside dimensions of Pilate's decision (and ours) on what to do with this One who radiates the "light of all people" (1:4).[2]

Scene 1 (18:29-32). Outside: Pilate and "the Jews"

"What accusation do you bring against this man?" (v. 29). The first conversation is between Pilate and the Jews, and it takes place outside Pilate's headquarters. At issue is who will be accountable for deciding the death penalty in Jesus' case. Pilate is ostensibly in charge of the trial, but he tries to extricate himself from the decision, which he regards as simply a parochial issue that is of little concern to the Roman government. The Jews respond by saying that Jesus has committed a capital crime, which requires a death penalty that Jewish law does not permit them to implement (cf. the description of the Sanhedrin's hearing in 11:46-53). They hand Jesus over for judgment.

Scene 2 (18:33-38a). Inside: Pilate and Jesus

"Are you the King of the Jews?" (v. 33). This question, which comprises part of Pilate's interrogation of Jesus inside his headquarters, presents the governing motif of the trial. The word "king" (*basileus*) occurs nine times in John's trial scene, the heaviest concentration of the word in the entire book.[3] The kingship question underscores the importance of religion and politics in the decision-making process. Political sedition poses a threat to the Roman government, and Pilate would be foolish to ignore such matters, for they pose a threat not only to the rule of his superiors in Rome but also to his own claim to power as the governor of Judea. Moreover, the Jewish leaders know

---

2. Here and throughout the subsequent discussion of these scenes, I draw from O'Day (ibid., 813–27). O'Day notes that the division into seven scenes is widely recognized by Johannine scholars. The most notable exception is R. Bultmann, who collapses 19:1-7 into a single scene (*The Gospel of John: A Commentary*, trans. G. Barclay, R. Beasley-Murray R. W. N. Hoare, J. K. Riches [Philadelphia: Westminster, 1971], 466). In effect, Bultmann's literary analysis only accentuates the creational echo, for it leaves unspoken the seventh and climatic scene, which anticipates but does not yet affirm the "very good" verdict that Genesis records.

3. John 18:33, 37 [2x], 39; 19:3, 12, 14, 15 [2x]; cf. 19:19, 21. Elsewhere only 4x (1:49; 6:15; 12:13, 15).

that if Rome believes they or their people are guilty of aiding or harboring a "terrorist," they will be held accountable. In other words, all those who bring Jesus to trial do so because it is both pragmatic and politically expedient.

But there is also a theological dimension to Pilate's question that should not be missed. His question—"I am not a Jew, am I?" (v. 35)—echoes that of the Pharisees in 9:40: "Surely we are not blind, are we?"[4] Both questions assume a negative response. Surely, Pilate is *not* a Jew; surely, the Pharisees are *not* so blind that they cannot see who Jesus is. And yet, ironically, both Pilate and the Pharisees *are* blind; in concert, both act like persons who are prepared to reject Jesus for self-interested, if prudent, reasons.

Scene 3 (18:38b-40). Outside: Pilate and "the Jews"

"Not this man, but Barabbas!" (v. 40). The previous scene (vv. 33-38a) ended with Pilate's question, "What is truth?" On the surface the question seems profound, but in John's account it is almost irrelevant. Pilate does not wait for an answer but instead perfunctorily exits the headquarters and returns outside to "the Jews." Once more, he tries to avoid further involvement in the case, for he still regards the "evidence" against Jesus to be either too little or too unimportant to merit his attention (v. 38b: "I find no case against him"). Once more, he suggests that the matter is strictly an internal issue for the Jews. They have a custom, apparently,[5] that allows them to release a prisoner at Passover. Perhaps they will choose to release Jesus, even if he is guilty of some violation of "Jewish" law. They do not cooperate. They ask for the release of one named Barabbas, presumably[6] a noted seditionist in his own right. Pilate's retreat to this option, and the preference of "the Jews" for it, indicates that neither is really interested in justice, for Barabbas should pose no less a threat to the government than Jesus, especially if he has already been tried and convicted of his crimes.

---

4. O'Day, "Gospel of John," 816–17.

5. The tradition about the release of Barabbas is found in all the Gospels, but there is no external attestation of the practice of a Passover release for criminals.

6. So the Synoptics (Matt 27:15-26; Mark 15:6-15; Luke 23:18:25) and Josephus (*J. W.* 2.253-254, 585).

The choice *for* Barabbas and *against* Jesus is freighted in ways that transcend its particular historical circumstances. As outsiders, we may be tempted to believe that we would have made different choices, choices more commendable, more indicative of our faith commitments. Like Pilate, we might say, "I am not a Jew, am I?" Like the Pharisees, we might say, "Surely, we are not blind, are we?" But like them, we should be cautious about joining the bandwagon in condemnation of those we think are so much less knowing than we. As George Herbert, the English priest and poet, reminds us, the story of the choices made by Pilate and the Jews may be "our story" as well:

> Thou who condemnest Jewish hate
> For choosing Barabbas a murderer
>   Before the Lord of Glory;
> Look back upon thine own estate,
> Call home thine eye (that busy wanderer)
>   *That choice may be thy story.*

> He that doth love, and love amiss
> This world's delights before true Christian joy,
>   Hath made a Jewish choice:
> The world an ancient murderer is;
>   Thousands of souls it hath and doth destroy
> With her enchanting voice.[7]

Scene 4 (19:1-3). Inside: Jesus and the Soldiers

"Hail, King of the Jews!" (19:3). Pilate returns inside, now to order Jesus beaten. Whereas the Synoptics place this scene at the end of the trial, just before the crucifixion, and depict it as a public act intended to mock and shame a condemned man, John places it in the middle of the trial, thus suggesting it is part of the normal legal process in arriving at a just verdict. Moreover, the purpose is not public mockery (it is done in private, outside the view of the crowd). Rather, John suggests that the flogging is ironically associated with Jesus' investiture as a king. The soldiers do not strip Jesus of his royal garments,

---

7. "Self-Condemnation," in J. Tobin, ed., *George Herbert: The Complete Poems* (London: Penguin Books, 2005), 160–61 (emphasis added).

then replace them after he has been beaten (cf. Matt 27:31; Mark 15:20). Instead, they robe him with royalty, then beat him as one who is (or claims to be) a king. From this point on in the trial, Jesus' appearance is an enigma that invites all who look on him to look carefully. His garments suggest royalty, but his body bears the scars of a common criminal. How can he possibly be regarded as a king who secures the safety of others if he cannot even protect himself against such violence and abuse?

As Pilate and the Jews *and we* ponder what we see in this beaten king, we may do so with the words of the prophet Isaiah in mind:

> Who has believed what we have heard? . . .
> he had no form or majesty that we should look at him,
>   nothing in his appearance that we should desire him.
> He was despised and rejected by others,
>   a man of suffering and acquainted with infirmity;
> and as one from whom others hide their faces
>   he was despised, and we held him of no account . . .
> Who could have imagined his future? (Isa 53:1, 2b-3, 8b)

Scene 5 (19:4-7). Outside: Pilate, Jesus, and "the Jews"

"Behold the Man" (19:5). Once again, the scene shifts to outside the headquarters, although now for the first time all the participants in the trial are together: Jesus, robed as a king, is silent, while Pilate and "the Jews" deliberate his fate. Pilate's words in verse 5—"Behold the man" (*ho anthrōpos*; NRSV: "Here is the man")—are perhaps the most famous and most discussed lines in the Gospel of John. They may be read on two levels.[8] On the level of the story line, they seem to convey the same disdain that Pilate has previously expressed for this parochial "Jewish" notion of kingship that has created such an unnecessary problem. On a second and deeper level, however, Pilate's words echo the description of Jesus elsewhere in the Fourth Gospel as "the Son of Man" (*ho huios tou anthrōpou*). This term is used not only with reference to Jesus' death (e.g., 3:14; 8:28; 12:23, 32-34) but also and perhaps still more tellingly to describe Jesus as the eschatological

---

8. O'Day, "Gospel of John," 819–20.

judge of the world (e.g., 5:27-28: "he [God] has given him [Jesus] authority to execute judgment, because he is the Son of Man. Do not be astonished at this; for the hour is coming when all who are in their graves will hear his voice and will come out—those who have done good, to the resurrection of life, and those who have done evil, to the resurrection of condemnation"). Thus Pilate, the political sovereign in Judea and the titular head of the judicial system, ironically presents Jesus as the *true* Judge.

From the perspective of both Pilate and "the Jews," what is at stake is a legal issue that binds both parties in different ways. As the governor of Judea, Pilate is required to secure the stability of the country, especially so as not to compromise the revenues it supplied to Rome. This means working within, even respecting, the local customs as much as possible, as long as they do not subvert Rome's ultimate authority. "The Jews" remind Pilate of this responsibility when they say, "We have a law, and according to that law he ought to die" (v. 7).[9] For his part, Pilate could hardly afford to be glib about his judicial authority, for herein lies not only his personal power to rule but also his representation of Rome's authority. In sum, bringing Jesus to trial and securing the appropriate verdict is the *legal thing to do*, for both Pilate and "the Jews."

Scene 6 (19:8-12). Inside: Pilate and Jesus (and "the Jews")

"You would have no power over me unless it had been given you from above" (19:11). Pilate retreats back inside his headquarters, and for the first time John describes his personal feelings about the process: "he was more afraid than ever" (v. 8). Why is he afraid? Perhaps because he has come to suspect that Jesus is indeed a holy man with connections that should make him wary (see further, below). The conversation between Pilate and Jesus that comprises this scene, however, suggests another reason. Pilate is concerned about *power*, specifically the power he possesses and seeks to exercise in the hope of winning Rome's favor and so advancing his career, and the

---

9. The allusion appears to be to the law against blasphemy, which prescribes death by stoning (Lev 24:13-16; cf. *Sanh.* 7.5). Luke reports that "the Jews" tried on two occasions to stone Jesus (8:59; 10:31), both times in connection with charges of blasphemy.

power that Jesus seems to think he has. Pilate's challenge to Jesus in v. 10—"Do you not know that I have power . . . to crucify you?"—recalls Jesus' words in 10:17-18: "No one takes it [my life] from me, but I lay it down of my own accord. I have power to lay it down, and I have power to take it up again." Now, Jesus tells Pilate that the titular power he claims for himself is an illusion. Jesus, a beaten man dressed in royal robes, claims that Pilate has only the power that "his father"—a Jewish God, no less!—gives him.

Verse 12 suggests that at this moment, just when Pilate has grown fearful, the carefully drawn boundaries between the outside and inside that he has constructed for himself collapse. Inside the headquarters and presumably out of sight of any who can see his indecisiveness, he tries once again to figure out how he can get out of this situation. Outside, "the Jews" seem to know his intentions before he speaks them, and their cries of protest penetrate his walls, as if they are standing in his own chambers. They prey on his worst political fears. If he releases Jesus, who claims to be a king, then he abdicates his duty to Rome. He will show himself unworthy of the title "Friend of the emperor," which appears to have been an official title awarded by Caesar to those who demonstrate loyalty and service to the empire. The "hour" of Pilate's decision about this man has now arrived.

Scene 7 (19:13-16a). Outside: Pilate, Jesus, and "the Jews"

"Here is your King!" (19:14). Back outside, once again in public view, Pilate announces his decision. It is now noon, on the Day of Preparation for Passover, the time when the Jewish regulations for Passover go into effect. At the very moment when the Jewish ritual invites the memory of God's power to deliver an abused people from slavery to freedom, when Jews reenact their belief in God's kingship, Pilate presents Jesus, God enfleshed, as "King of the Jews." He is beaten, robed in royal purple, crowned with thorns, and placed on the "judge's bench," as if to suggest, ironically, that Jesus is now positioned to effect the very liberation from oppressive rule for which the Jews have long waited. Pilate's hour of decision coincides with that of the crowd who beholds this would-be king. The response of the Jewish leadership? "We have no king but the emperor" (v. 15). With these words, one of the central affirmations of the Passover ritual is

nullified. Note the following hymn from a typical Passover seder in first-century Palestine:

> From everlasting to everlasting thou art God
> Beside thee we have no king, redeemer, or savior,
> No liberator, deliverer, provider
> None who takes pity in every time of distress and trouble
> We have no king but thee.[10]

The trial of Jesus is now complete. The last words of the seventh and final scene are, "Then he [Pilate] handed him over to them to be crucified" (19:16). John's seven scenes echo the seven-day creational pattern of Genesis 1. The idea that Jesus' trial has creational ramifications recalls and accents the Prologue's invitation to understand that this story has cosmic, not just local, reverberations. In sum, Jesus' trial, especially Pilate's tremorous instruction—"Behold the man"— is both literal and metaphorical. Jesus is literally on trial for his life. On a deeper level and more important, John suggests, *the world is on trial for its life*.[11] At the hour of decision, when the world hopes and expects to hear the divine verdict "very good" (Gen 1:31), John reports that the world, Jews and Gentiles in one accord, say instead, "Crucify him! Crucify him!" (19:6; cf. 19:15, 16).

II. LOOKING AT PILATE LOOKING AT JESUS

I invite you to ponder the role of Pilate in John's trial scene. For my purposes here, Pilate represents the onlooker, the one who looks on and invites us to look on Jesus—to "behold the man"—as if the decision that must be made about who he is is ours as well. The decision we make about Pilate, indeed the choice anyone makes to "hand Jesus over" to the powers that be, as G. Herbert reminds us, is *our story* too.

John portrays Pilate as a person caught in the tension between internal quandary and external expectations. In the privacy of his quarters, where no one can see him, he engages Jesus with questions

---

10. W. Meeks, *The Prophet-King: Moses Traditions and the Johannine Christology* (Leiden: E. J. Brill, 1967), 71.

11. O'Day, "The Gospel of John," 826 (emphasis added).

that betray both idle curiosity and trepidation. On the one hand, he does not want to be distracted from important responsibilities by trivial pursuits that waste his time. On the other, he dare not jeopardize his career by unwittingly allowing any issue, however trivial it may seem, to become a major political liability. His ambitions require that he address each and every decision he makes by calculating the personal and political consequences. In religious terms, he must decide whether it is better for his career that he be viewed as a saint or a sinner. The ambivalence of the post-biblical assessment of Pilate may cause us to wonder whether the promise of either of these two options is compelling.

Apart from the Gospels and the first-century Jewish historians Josephus and Philo, we know little about Pontius Pilate. The basic facts are these.[12] He was the fifth and longest serving (26–37 CE) Roman governor of Judea. His title "Prefect" suggests that he possessed military power, but while there were certainly troops at his disposal, it is likely that they functioned more as police than as military forces. For serious military maneuvers, Pilate depended on the legate of Syria, who had four legions of troops at his disposal. There are no records of the legate of Syria's involvement in Palestine during Pilate's tenure, which suggests that his ten-year rule of Judea was generally quiet and peaceful.[13]

Pilate's primary responsibilities were administrative. First, and most important, he was the head of the judicial system (Josephus uses the phrase "with power even to execute" to refer to his authority; *J.W.* 2.8; *Ant.* 18.1). The only details concerning Pilate as judge come from the New Testament accounts of Jesus' trial. Pilate's other main administrative duties were fiscal: "he was responsible for the collection of tributes and taxes, for the proper disbursement of funds for provincial needs, and for the forwarding to Rome of revenues and reports."[14] Here too we have few details about Pilate's exercise

---

12. On Pilate, see D. Schwartz, "Pontius Pilate," *ABD*, vol. 5, 395–401; H. Bond, *Pontius Pilate in History and Tradition* (New York: Cambridge University Press, 1998); W. Carter, *Pontius Pilate: Portraits of a Roman Governor* (Collegeville, MN: Liturgical Press, 2003).

13. Schwartz, "Pontius Pilate," 397.

14. Ibid.

of these duties, apart from Josephus's report that Pilate used Jewish temple funds to construct an aqueduct to bring water to Jerusalem, a decision that provoked Jewish opposition (*J. W.* 2.175-177; *Ant.* 18.60-62; see the oblique references to "the insurrection" led by Barabbas in Mark 15:7 and Luke 23:19, which may refer to this event).

In general, Pilate's rule of Judea seems to have been relatively tranquil, with little more than sporadic and mostly minor incidents of local unrest. Two such incidents receive mention in extra-biblical sources. First, Josephus and Philo report that Pilate introduced into Jerusalem imperial standards bearing the image of the Roman emperor Tiberius, which aroused such Jewish protest on religious grounds that Pilate was forced to remove the offending items to Caesarea (Josephus, *J. W.* 2.169-174; *Ant.* 18.55-59; cf. Philo, *Embassy* 209-305).[15] [FIGURE 1.1]

The second is an incident that appears to have contributed to Pilate's removal from office. Josephus reports that in 37 CE Pilate used violence to put down an armed demonstration by Samaritans at Mt. Gerizim, then executed a number of their leaders (*Ant.* 18.85-87). A Samaritan delegation complained to Vitellius, the legate of Syria, who responded by suspending Pilate from office and dispatching him to Rome for disciplining (*Ant.* 18.88-89).[16] Pilate never returned and ultimately died in Rome in unknown circumstances. Eusebius claims that Pilate committed suicide in 39 CE (*Hist. eccl.* 2.7). In other hagiographical accounts, Pilate was either exiled or executed.[17]

So what are we to make of Pilate? How should we regard him and his governorship of Judea? More important, who was this man who supervised the trial of Jesus and presented him to the crowd *and to us* with the words, "Behold the man"? These words, fossilized in the Latin translation *Ecce homo*, have long outlived him. Since at least the Middle Ages, they have been an enormously influential thematic

---

15. Ibid., 399; Carter, *Pontius Pilate*, 13–14.

16. Schwartz, "Pontius Pilate," 398; Carter, *Pontius Pilate*, 14.

17. T. Grüll, "The Legendary Fate of Pontius Pilate," *Classica et Mediaevalia* 61 (2010): 151–76. For images of Pilate's death in medieval art and iconography, see C. Hourihane, *Pontius Pilate, Anti-Semitism and the Passion in Medieval Art* (Princeton: Princeton University Press, 2009), 316–17 (Figures 156, 157).

FIGURE 1.1

Pilate sits on a throne bearing two square pictures of Tiberius. He considers the case against Jesus (far left) presented by Caiaphas, the high priest (with white beard, middle left).

Sixth-century illuminated Greek MS. Rossano, Italy. (Credit: The Yorck Project [2002]; *10.000 Meisterwerke der Malerei* [DVD-ROM], distributed by Directmedia Publishing GmbH, GNU Free)

catchword for Christian art and iconography.[18] So what are we to see and understand when we look at Pilate looking at Jesus? [FIGURE 1.2]

With good reason, Pilate has long had a terrible reputation. All of the Gospels describe him as something of a coward. He seems to recognize that Jesus' trial is a gross miscarriage of justice, yet he lacks

FIGURE 1.2

Robed in the regalia of his power, Pilate's royal staff is inscribed with the words that have come to define his role in history: *Ecce Homo*.

Anonymous. *Pontius Pilate*. 16th century. Museo dell'Accademia, Venice. (Credit: Cameraphoto Arte, Venice / Art Resource, NY)

18. See especially the extensive discussion in Hourihane, *Pontius Pilate*.

the courage to use his power as the governor of Judea to stop it. John, for example, portrays him as a simple man caught between moral scruples and political expectations. Unable to negotiate between the scruples of his conscience and the demands of his office, he simply washes his hands of the whole affair, claims he is "innocent of this man's blood" (so Matt 27:24), and hands Jesus over to crucifixion. The Jewish historians Josephus and Philo generally extend this negative portrayal by emphasizing that Pilate was a ruthless and mean-spirited small-time despot whose only goal in life was to advance his career at the expense of a hapless people. Philo's characterization is a case in point. He describes Pilate's administration as one defined by "his venality, his violence, his thefts, his assaults, his abusive behavior, his frequent executions of untried prisoners, and his endless savage ferocity" (*Embassy* 302).[19]

Against this backdrop, it is interesting to note that early Christians gradually began to depict Pilate in a different way, not as a notorious sinner who executed Christ but instead as something of a hero, an active agent in advancing God's work, indeed as a saint. Tertullian (ca. 200), for example, claims to know of a tradition in which Pilate sent letters to the emperor Tiberius that contained detailed accounts of the wonderful deeds Jesus performed (*Apol.* 5, 21). He is convinced by the tone of the correspondence that Pilate "became already a Christian in his conscience" (*Apol.* 21-24). Eusebius reports that Pilate became a Christian and tried to convert Tiberius to Christianity (*Hist. eccl.* 11.2). A fourth-century relief suggests that Pilate was a disciple-like convert to Christianity. [FIGURE 1.3] At least by the fourth century, iconographic images on sarcophagi depict Pilate as among (or at least associated with) biblical heroes of faith, especially Abraham and Daniel. [FIGURE 1.4]

Tertullian, Eusebius, and other early Christian accounts are the source for a rich tradition of stories that embellish the legend of Pilate's goodness. A fifth-century account, "The Giving Up of Pontius Pilate," reports that Caesar ordered a captain named Albius to cut off Pilate's head as punishment for his mismanagement of Judea. Hearing the judgment, Pilate prayed to God for deliverance.

---

19. For a comparison of the perspectives of "Philo's Pilate" and "Josephus's Pilate," see Carter, *Pontius Pilate*, 15–17.

FIGURE 1.3

The leftmost panel depicts Jesus washing the disciples' feet. Directly opposite this panel (rightmost), Pilate extends his hands to be washed. Both scenes symbolize baptism, innocence, and the forgiveness of sins.

Fourth-century relief. Antiquities Museum. Arles, France. (Credit: Wikimedia Commons, PD-US)

And, behold, when Pilate had finished his prayer, there came a voice from heaven, saying: "*All the generations and families of the nations shall count thee blessed, because under thee have been fulfilled all those things said about me by the prophets; and thou thyself shalt be seen as my witness at my second appearing, when I shall judge the tribes of Israel, and those that have not owned my name.*" And the prefect struck off the head of Pilate; and, behold, an angel of the Lord received it. And his wife Procla, seeing the angel coming and receiving the head, being filled with joy herself also, immediately gave up the ghost, and was buried along with her husband (emphasis added).[20]

The *Martyrium Pilati* ("On the Death of Pilate") provides a similar account, with considerable embellishment of Pilate's own

---

20. For the text of "The Giving Up of Pontius Pilate," see A. Roberts, J. Donaldson, eds., *The Anti-Nicene Fathers* (Grand Rapids: Eerdmans, 1986), vol. 6, 464–65. See further, Grüll, "The Legendary Fate of Pontius Pilate," 151–76. On the history of the legends that detached Pilate from Herod, disassociated him from the Jews, and revered him as a saint, see A. Mingana, "The Lament of the Virgin" and "The Martyrdom of Pilate," in *Woodbrooke Studies* 2 (1928): 163–77.

FIGURE 1.4

A 4th-century sarcophagus in the Vatican depicts *Jesus before Pilate* (far right), who is washing hands. Opposite, far left, is a panel depicting *Abraham and Isaac*. The pairing highlights similarities between two virtuous figures, *Pilate and Abraham*, both of whom were required, against their wishes, to preside at the sacrifice of an innocent person.

Carrara marble sarcophagus from the end of the 4th century representing the handing over of the law to Saint Peter. (Credit: Wikimedia Commons, CCA-SA4.0)

crucifixion and resurrection. According to this legend, the Roman emperor ordered Pilate to be crucified on the cross upon which Jesus had died. Those gathered around the cross shouted, "O Pilate, disciple of Jesus of Nazareth, if your Master has risen up from the dead, come down from the cross, and we will believe in Him." Pilate then prays,

> O my Lord, I have polluted your holy cross by the hanging of my body on it, because it is a pure wood and my body is an impure body; your blood is an innocent blood, and my blood is carnal. . . . Have pity on me, your sinning servant, who has been lifted up on your holy cross, as I am not worthy of all these benefits. I do not sigh because of my nudity, but I weep for your deep humility and self-effacement. Now I ask you, O my Lord Jesus Christ, not in my own name, but for the glory of your Majesty and the honor of your cross, to grant rest and a happy lot to my poor soul. Grant rest to

me, your servant Pilate, to your maidservant Procula, and to my
children, in the day in which you will come to judge the world.[21]

The Jews rail and scoff at Pilate and Procula, who kisses her husband's
legs as he hangs from the cross; then they are silenced by a voice from
heaven that announces God's intention to save Pilate:

> Then two crowns came down from heaven, equal to each other
> in glory and majesty, and a voice from heaven was heard saying:
> "Know O Pilate and Procula, that you will be crowned with these
> two crowns that came down to you from Heaven, because of the
> sufferings you have borne for your God and your great faith in
> Him. Then the two crowns disappeared and went up to heaven.[22]

Pilate was never canonized as such, but Coptic and Ethiopian
churches regard Pilate and his wife (cf. Matt 27:19) as saints.[23] The
Ethiopian Church, for example, commemorates Saint Pilate on June
25 with a liturgical text that absolves both Pilate and his wife of
responsibility for Jesus' death:

> Salutation to Pilate who washed his hands
> so he himself was pure of the blood of Christ
> and salutation to Procula, his wife,
> who sent him the message: "Do not condemn Him"
> because that man is pure and just.[24]

Ethiopian effigy poems celebrate the story with rhetorical flourish.

---

21. For text and translation, see A. Mingana, ed., "Martyrdom of Pilate," *Bulletin of the John Rylands Library* 12 (1928): 258–59.

22. Ibid., 259.

23. Cf. E. Cerulli, "La légende de l'emperur Tibère et de Pilate dans deux nouveaux documents éthiopens," *Byzantion* 36 (1966): 26–34; L. Luìsier, "De Pilate chez les Coptes," *Orientalia Christiana Periodica* 62 (1996): 411–25. On the portrayals of Pilate's wife, see R. Mellinkoff, "Pilate's Wife," in J. F. Hamburger, A. S. Korteweg, eds., *Tributes in Honor of James H. Morrow: Studies in Painting and Manuscript Illumination of the Late Middle Ages and Northern Renaissance* (London/ Turnhout: Brepols Publishers, 2006), 337–41.

24. E. Cerulli, "Tiberius and Pontius Pilate in Ethiopian Tradition and Poetry," *Proceedings of the British Academy, London* 59 (1973): 148.

Salutation to thy neck, O Pilate, soldier and magistrate of Rome,
crowned with thorns like the Master, the Nazarene.
When the descendants of Simon and Levi afflicted thee,
no worldly thought troubled thee.
Salutation to thy shoulders which had carried the Cross,
and to thy back, wounded by the scourge of the Jews;
O Pilate, because thine ascetic struggles had been very good,
the Lord, whom thou hast scourged, desisted from vengeance
and sent food to thee from Heaven.[25]

The Christian rehabilitation of Pilate might have been a fairly harmless interpretive move had it not coincided with the growing anti-Jewishness of the increasingly Gentile church. At least from the time of Constantine, the move to absolve Pilate, the Gentile, of any wrongdoing in the matter of Jesus' death helped to legitimate the (Christian) state and the Christian church to which it was inextricably linked for both political and religious reasons. Regrettably, sadly, this legitimation crystallized around the charge that "the Jews"—not Pilate, not the Gentiles—killed Jesus. The seedbed for this anti-Jewish polemic, it must be admitted, is the New Testament itself, especially the Gospels, which reflect the growing antipathy in the first century between Christians and Jews. Mark 15:10, for example, purports to know Pilate's private thoughts when it says, "He perceived that it was out of jealousy that the chief priests had handed him [Jesus] over." Why should the Gospel writer want us to think that the chief priests—not Pilate—were the real instigators of the trial that led to Jesus' death? Other examples might be cited, but one further text may be singled out for special mention, because it has such enormous influence on our cultural assumptions. Matthew 27:24-25 describes Pilate's hand-washing scene with these words:

So when Pilate saw that he could do nothing, but rather that a riot was beginning, he took some water and washed his hands before the crowd, saying, "I am innocent of this man's blood; see to it

---

25. Ibid., 152. An "effigy" poem (Ethiopic *malke*) is a multi-strophied poem that celebrates every part of the body of the one being exalted. The rhetorical effect is to present a full-body image of the holy person. For the complete poem, "Effigies of Pilate," see ibid., 150–54.

yourselves." Then the people as a whole answered, "His blood be on us and on our children!" So he released Barabbas for them; and after flogging Jesus, he handed him over to be crucified.

These words do not record history. They record Matthew's perspective on a time when Jews and Christians were locked in acrimonious debate. Matthew's take on this is that "all the people" (read Jewish people) who rejected Jesus are responsible for what happened to him. Thus a pretext for Christian persecution of Jews was set. [FIGURE 1.5]

FIGURE 1.5

The Hungarian artist Munkasy depicts the crowd's demand for Jesus' blood. Pilate listens skeptically to the charges presented against Jesus by the high priest Caiaphas (white turban and beard). A man from the crowd raises his arms in support of the charges, as if in the act of uttering the words, "His blood be on us and on our children" (Matt 27:25).

Mihaly Munkasy. *Christ before Pilate.* 1881. Oil on canvas. Hungarian National Gallery. (Credit: Wikimedia Commons, PD-old)

A strong case can be made in support of the argument that Matthew's words—"His blood be on us and on our children"— have contributed to (or caused) more violence against Jews, more bloodshed, than any other verse in the Bible.[26] The evidence we must reckon with is centuries of anti-Semitism, pogroms, and the murder of six million Jews under Hitler's Nazi regime during the Holocaust. The stereotype of Jews as bloodthirsty Christ killers was nowhere more dramatically enshrined in culture than in the Passion plays that emerged in the early fourteenth century, especially in France and Germany. Passion plays, a dramatic reenactment of the Mass, enabled local citizens to participate directly in the drama the Gospels reported.

As local affairs, performed and directed by members of the community, Passion plays were a matter of pride for those who staged them. They were eventually treated as festivals, sometimes running three or more days in length. Since they were about Jesus' Passion, literally his "suffering" (Latin, *passio*), they concentrated on the reenactment of Jesus' trial and execution. And since the Gospels mostly depict the Jews negatively in these scenes, the Passion plays traditionally featured exaggerated caricatures of Jews as clamoring for Jesus' blood. As a result, they often stirred up Jewish hatred, even sparking pogroms or massacres of Jews. With good reason, "Holy Week" has historically been one of the most dangerous times on the calendar for Jews to be on the streets.[27]

The longest-running and best-known Passion play has been performed in the Bavarian village of Oberammergau every ten years since 1634. It originated as the town's fulfillment of a promise to God in exchange for being spared from the plague of that year. Like other Passion plays, the Oberammergau play contained, until recently

---

26. See, for example, Amy-Jill Levine, "Holy Week and the Hatred of the Jews: How to Avoid Anti-Judaism this Easter," ABC Religion and Ethics, abc.net.au/ religion/holy-week-and-the-hatred-of-the-jews/11029900. Posted April 2019. For a fuller exploration of the subject, see A.-J. Levine, *The Misunderstood Jew: The Church and the Scandal of the Jewish Jesus* (New York: HarperCollins, 2007), 87–118.

27. In 1539, for example, Pope Paul III banned the annual Passion plays in Rome because they had regularly incited violence and riots against the Jewish quarter of the city.

(see below), vicious characterizations of Jews that went far beyond the Gospel accounts; the blood curse in Matt 27:25, for example, was repeated several times during the performance. When Hitler saw the 300th anniversary of the Oberammergau play in 1934, he commended it as a "convincing portrayal of the menace of Jewry" and a "precious tool" in the fight against Judaism.

In 1988, the National Conference of Catholic Bishops, in compliance with the Vatican Commission for Religious Relations with the Jews, published a new set of guidelines for the portrayal of Jesus' Passion ("Criteria for the Evaluation of Dramatizations of the Passion").[28] The guidelines explain, "The overall aim of any depiction of the passion should be the unambiguous presentation of the doctrinal understanding of the event in light of faith: . . . 'Christ in his boundless love freely underwent his passion and death because of the sins of all, so that all might attain salvation'." With respect to the question of who bears responsibility for Jesus' death, which the Passion plays had conventionally assigned to the Jews, the guidelines cite the *Catechism* of the Council of Trent in calling for "a profound examination of our own guilt, through sin, for Jesus' death":

> In this guilt are involved all those who fall frequently into sin; for, as our sins consigned Christ the Lord to the death of the cross, most certainly those who wallow in sin and iniquity crucify to themselves again the Son of God . . . . This guilt seems more enormous in us than in the Jews since, if they had known it, they would never have crucified the Lord of glory; while we, on the contrary, professing to know him, yet denying him by our actions, seem in some sort to lay violent hands on him.

To achieve these goals, the guidelines recommend that Passion portrayals show the complexity of the Jewish world of Jesus' time. For example, they should refrain from picturing Jesus or his teachings in false opposition to the Jews collectively or even to groups like

---

28. "Criteria for the Evaluation of Dramatizations of the Passion: Bishops' Committee for Ecumenical and Interreligious Affairs National Conference of Catholic Bishops," usccb.org/beliefs-and-teachings/ecumenical-and-interreligious/jewish/upload/Criteria-for-the-Evaluation-of-Dramatizations-of-the-Passion-1988.pdf (accessed July 2020).

the Pharisees. And they should avoid caricaturing the Jews "as avaricious (e.g., in Temple money-changer scenes); blood thirsty (e.g., in certain depictions of Jesus' appearance before the Temple priesthood or before Pilate); or implacable enemies of Christ (e.g., by changing the 'small' crowd at the governor's palace into a teeming mob)."

On first thought, we might suppose that such guidelines have been effective. The script of the Oberammergau Passion play no longer contains the blood curse in Matthew. And at the Last Supper, Jesus and his disciples wear prayer shawls, which shows more clearly their Jewish identity. On closer inspection, however, we have cause to wonder whether anything much has changed. Mel Gibson's 2004 movie, *Passion of the Christ*, evoked wide-ranging rebuke from media, the US Conference of Catholic Bishops, and the Anti-Defamation League (a Jewish organization) for its unambiguously exaggerated portrayal of the Jews as a bloodthirsty mob who were ultimately responsible for Jesus' crucifixion. Amy-Jill Levine, a prominent Jewish New Testament scholar, is blunt in arguing that the "real problem with 'Passion'" is its passionate anti-Jewish polemic, which she likens to Hitler's reign of terror. She cites three examples from the movie that she fears will extend, exacerbate, and lend cultural endorsement to such anti-Semitism. (1) The unbiblical claim that Jesus' cross was manufactured in the temple is "analogous to asserting that the ovens of Auschwitz were constructed in the Vatican, under the supervision of Pius XII." (2) Pilate, the Roman governor, is portrayed as manipulated by the High Priest, Caiaphas, which suggests that "these poor Nazi occupiers of mid-20th century Rome could not resist Vatican pressure to rid the city of Jews." (3) The movie repeatedly shows bloodthirsty Jews torturing Jesus, whereas the Romans, a preternaturally compassionate people, needed Satan's promptings. "This is tantamount to saying that 'the Jews' in Dachau tortured fellow Jews just because they felt like it, whereas the Nazis needed supernatural incitement."[29] Such criticism notwithstanding, Gibson's movie

---

29. Amy-Jill Levine, "The Real Problem with 'Passion,'" beliefnet.com/story/130/story_13051.html. For an account of the critique of the movie by representatives from United States Conference of Bishops, the Anti-Defamation League, and an ad hoc group of Jewish and Christian New Testament scholars, see P. Fredriksen, "Mad Mel: The Gospel According to Gibson," *The New Republic*, July 28, 2003. Available online: newrepublic.com/article/134166/mad-mel (accessed July 2020).

grossed more than 600 million dollars, plus approximately 75 million dollars more for merchandising a wide range of products, including "Passion of Christ nail necklaces."

You will have to judge for yourselves whether and how culturally engrained anti-Jewish and anti-Semitic attitudes shape our journey during this Lenten season. My objective here is only to suggest that when Pilate presents Jesus to the crowd with the words, "Behold the man," he summons us each and every one, perhaps unwittingly, to think very carefully about *how* we see, and *why* we see, the suffering of an innocent person the way we do.

III. THE "ART" OF SUFFERING

I began this presentation with a series of questions that might plot our Lenten journey. How are we to respond to Pilate's summons, "Behold the man"? If we place ourselves in the crowd to whom Pilate presents Jesus, what are we supposed to see and know when we look on this beaten and condemned innocent man? Let me conclude by now placing this question in the context of another: what do we learn from looking at the "art" of suffering? My use of the word "art" with respect to the idea of suffering has a double meaning.

On the one hand, it refers to the visual representation of pain and suffering, for example, the paintings, etchings, sculptures, and photographs that professional artists provide for our viewing. The representations are external to us; we look at them from the outside. We may appreciate them because they are pleasant to behold; we may dislike them because they do not please us aesthetically.[30] We like Rembrandt's work, for example, because its subject matter is familiar and its composition is pleasing to the eye, but not the work

---

In the aftermath of the movie's release, many book-length discussions appeared. See, for example, Z. Garber, ed., *Mel Gibson's Passion: The Film, the Controversy, and Its Implications* (Shofar Supplements in Jewish Studies; West Lafayette, IN: Perdue University Press, 2006). Gibson's sequel to the 2004 movie, *The Passion of Christ: The Resurrection*, is scheduled for release in 2021.

30. For discussion of the ways we "traffic in pain" by aestheticizing "beautiful" images of pain and suffering, see M. Reinhardt, H. Edwards, eds., *Beautiful Suffering: Photography and the Traffic in Pain* (Chicago: University of Chicago Press/Williamstown, MA: Williams College Museum of Art, 2007). See especially the lead essay by M. Reinhardt, "Traffic in Pain," 7–12.

of Jackson Pollack, which is too wild, too incomprehensible, too modern or vulgar for our tastes. Either way, when we look on art that depicts suffering at this level, we usually do not attach any moral charge to what we see. We are mostly unflinching voyeurs.[31]

On the other hand, the word "art" suggests the possibility that there is an art *to* or *in* suffering, that by looking at and thinking about the depictions of the agony of others, we may learn something about the nature of suffering that applies to us in a personal way. Is there an art to suffering? A right way and a wrong way to do it? Do we embrace some models of suffering, whether instinctively or upon reflection, as noble, virtuous, and commendable, something we might accept, even welcome, if we are convicted the cause is righteous? One thinks, for example, of Gandhi, Nelson Mandela, Martin Luther King Jr., or countless others who gave themselves up to martyrdom for others. Are other examples of suffering models we shun, perhaps even condemn, because they strike us as cowardly, self-serving, or simply wrong? Surely some suffering, however regrettable, is not only predictable but also necessary, for as both religion and law remind us, immoral or illegal acts have consequences: the righteous/innocent will prosper; the wicked/guilty will be punished. One thinks, for example, of convicted terrorists like Timothy McVeigh or Khalid Sheikh Mohammed, or Saddam Hussein, who was convicted by an Iraqi court of crimes against humanity. At this level, viewing the art of suffering is more than an external exercise; it is a process of first internalizing ideas and emotions drawn from what we have seen and felt, then of knowing that we are somehow admonished or inspired to act on what is churning in our insides. We may be summoned to join the struggle against what we perceive has caused the suffering, or we may feel compelled to add our voice in support of the principle that justifies the punishment we feel is right or necessary. Either way, at this level, we cannot look at the art of suffering as mere spectators. We flinch in the presence of its moral claim on us.

Alongside the proliferation of meditational and devotional writings in the Middle Ages that took up the theme of Christ's sufferings

---

31. I draw here upon the work of S. Sontag, *Regarding the Pain of Others* (New York: Farrar, Straus, and Giroux, 2003), especially chapter 3, to which I will return in the third presentation (chapter 3).

(e.g., Anselm of Canterbury, *Cur Deus Homo?* [11th century], Thomas à Kempis, *Imitatio Christi* [15th century]), the *Ecce Homo* theme became a marked feature in the art and iconography of culture. Bosch and Dürer set precedents for treatments of the subject by Titian, Corregio, Tintoretto, Rubens, and Rembrandt, among many others. The sheer number of these renderings has made a virtual genre of the subject, such that the *Latin* words I have used for the title of this presentation are a part of our *English* lexicon. When we hear them, we do not need a dictionary to have a picture in our mind of Christ wearing a crown of thorns.

The question I have been circling around since I began the presentation is this: What are we supposed to see when we look at these pictures? To this question I have now added the suggestion that viewing the "art" of suffering is both an external and internal process of discernment. We can be spectators or participants; we can look for aesthetic fulfillment and walk away satisfied, or we can feel a moral compulsion that cannot be satisfied until we act on it. In short, we can flinch before what we see and understand, or not.[32] Our inside-outside options may not be different from those John assigns to Pilate, who finds that his decision about what to do with the Christ who stands before him requires an uneasy back-and-forth movement between private thoughts and public responsibilities.

I am at the end of this presentation, but let me set the table for what lies ahead by inviting you to look on three pictures with the questions and thoughts above in mind. "Behold the man" . . . see what you see, think what you think, feel what you feel, and decide for yourselves whether it is enough merely to look or if something more is necessary.

Tintoretto's elongated, twisting figures and the flickering, unsteady light in his paintings reflect the influence of El Greco. [FIGURE 1.6] In *Christ Before Pilate*, Tintoretto draws the viewers' attention to the slender, motionless Christ, who stands before Pilate.

---

32. For discussion of an "ethics of vision" that is committed to face the pain and suffering displayed in images, such as a photograph of a person with HIV/AIDS, see M. Bal, "The Pain of Images," *Journal of Visual Culture* 4 (2005): 145–62. On the dilemma of flinching or not flinching when looking at images of pain and suffering, see F. Möller, "The Looking/Not Looking Dilemma," *Review of International Studies* 35 (2009): 781–94.

Christ, haloed by the sign of divinity, is cloaked not in the colors of royalty but in the white of innocence. Pilate, robed in red but uncrowned, sits on the royal throne of judgment, washing his hands to symbolize his innocence, yet he turns his face away from the verdict he has delivered, as if acknowledging with his body, if not his mind, that his innocence is not equal to that of the One who stands before him. The crowd who circles the throne and provides the audience for what is happening shows mixed but largely benign reactions. Some

FIGURE 1.6

Tintoretto (1519–1594). *Christ Before Pilate*. 1566–1567. Oil on canvas. Scuola Grande di San Rocco, Venice. (Credit: Wikimedia Commons, PD-US)

look toward the judgment scene; some look down; some look away. A scribe to Pilate's left seems preoccupied with recording the facts, as if nothing else is required of him.[33]

In Quentin Massys's *Ecce Homo*, a disinterested Pilate hands over Jesus to be crucified. [FIGURE 1.7] He does not look on the One he has sentenced, even though he stands next to him on a balcony so crowded that people's arms are touching. A soldier, mouth wide open with mockery, places a scarlet cloak over the shoulders of Jesus.

FIGURE 1.7

Quentin Massys (Metsys) (1466–1530). *Ecce Homo* or *Christ Presented to the People*. c. 1515. Color on wood. Museo de Prado, Madrid. (Credit: Wikimedia Commons/The Yorck Project)

---

33. See further T. Nichols, *Jacopo Tintoretto* (Grove Art Essentials; Oxford: Oxford University Press, 2016).

A man to Jesus' left tugs on the noose around his neck. He looks out on the crowd, jaw jutted with determination and satisfaction. His garments are common, suggesting that he has somehow crawled out from the crowd below where he belongs and up onto the balcony, so that he can be part of the action. Above and to the right of Jesus' head, a stone sculpture depicts a mother cradling a baby, perhaps suggesting that every mother would wish to protect her child from a life that might end up like the one playing out just below. Other children gather at her feet, as if eager to be included in her protective clutches, but three are already precariously (or curiously) close to being over the edge of safety. Whether they will climb closer to her safety or fall into the chaos below is uncertain.[34]

Hieronymous Bosch's *The Crowning with Thorns* presses us to still another level of viewing and thinking. [FIGURE 1.8] One commentator has observed, "Bosch was to diabolical painting what Henry Ford became to the automobile. He didn't invent it, but after he got involved the product was never the same again."[35] Bosch seems to have been haunted by the mindless cruelty of human beings and the fascinating vitality of true ugliness. Even sadistic monsters, he seemed to suggest, sometimes seem troublingly human. One thinks, for example, of our abiding fascination with R. L. Stevenson's *The Strange Case of Dr. Jekyll and Mr. Hyde* (1866), which teases us to laugh about the ever-present good-evil aspect of human character. Bosch seems intent on showing how people in crowds, onlookers, may be caught up in violence, as if succumbing to a seizure, an irresistible impulse triggered by the mere proximity to cruelty. One such example is this depiction of four persons who malevolently eye the convicted and now vulnerable Christ. Whatever their "normal" status in life may have been before this incident, they each have now become part of the drama. The man at bottom left, with a grossly elongated nose, wears a headdress with the crescent-and-star of Islam,

34. See further J. K. G. Shearman, *Only Connect: Art and the Spectator in the Italian Renaissance* (A. W. Mellon Lectures in the Fine Arts, 1998; Washington, D.C.: National Gallery of Art/Princeton: Princeton University Press, 1992), 38, Figures 31, 32.

35. T. Foote, *The World of Bruegel, c. 1525–1569* (New York: Time-Life Books, 1968), 42.

FIGURE 1.8

Hieronymus Bosch (1450–1516). *The Crowning with Thorns.* ...c. 1479–1516. Oil on oak panel. National Gallery, London. (Credit: Wikimedia Commons, PD–US)

which identifies him as an Arab who cannot pass up this chance to
berate a Jew. The man at the top left, with gauntleted right arm,
places a crown of thorns on Jesus' head. His face is impassive, as
if he simply happened onto the scene and decided to lend a disinterested hand. The arrow through his cap suggests that he will be
eternally damned for not thinking more carefully about the decisions
he makes. The man at the top right wears a spiked collar, symbolizing
his role as a professional executioner. This is merely his job; he crin-
kles up his face as if to say that he must earn a living, no matter how
distasteful the requirements may be. The man at the bottom right
is nondescript; perhaps he is merely a passerby who is caught up in
the moment. He reaches for Jesus' heart, and by doing so he adds his
hands to those of others who are ready to take a life. The four are all
"others," unknown people in a crowd from a time long ago.[36] Even
so, Bosch seems to be asking us to look at what he has painted and
then ask ourselves, which one of these are you?

With this last unthinkable question—Which one of these are
you?—I leave you to think about the Lenten journey we have only
just begun. When we read the text and see the pictures that exegete
the words *Ecce Homo*, "Behold the man," what do we *see*? What do
we *feel*? What must we *do*? As we ponder these questions, a reminder
from John's Gospel: it is not only Pilate or the crowd that gathered
around him in the first century that is on trial. It is the whole world,
which having looked once more at the God-enfleshed Word, bruised,
full of grace and truth, must now decide how to respond.

---

36. See further M. Ilsink, J. Koldeweij, *Hieronymus Bosch: Visions of Genius*
(New Haven: Yale University Press, 2016), 54–77 and Figure 13; P. Vanden-
broeck, "Hieronymus Bosch," *Grove Art Online, Oxford Art Online* (Oxford:
Oxford University Press), doi.org/10.1093/gao/9781884446054.article.T010250
(accessed July 2020).

2

"Look at My Hands and Feet . . . . Touch Me and See"

Our Lenten journey is instructed by two imperatives. Pilate speaks the first one, which we explored in the first presentation (chapter 1). At the end of John's Gospel, having handed over to the crowd a beaten and condemned Jesus, Pilate says, "Behold the man." We looked at Pilate looking at Jesus and asked ourselves what are we supposed to see and know when we look on this scene. Viewed through Pilate's eyes, we are onlookers, persons whose roles in this drama allow us to make our decisions from a safe distance. As we weigh the personal and public consequences of the choices before us, what will we decide when Pilate hands Jesus over to us? Will we be practical? If so, we will find a way to get the consent of our conscience to join the crowd, because to do anything else puts us at odds with Rome and jeopardizes our best chance for prosperity. We know we must go along to get along. Or will we flinch before the sight of this innocent man, so bruised and broken? Will pangs of conscience compel us to intervene on his behalf, perhaps to separate ourselves from the crowd by yelling out, "Stop! This is not right!"? If so, we will set our compass by moral convictions instead of self-interests, even if it means we may lose more than we gain. In the space between us and Jesus, now objectified as an uninvited problem that has been imposed on our lives, the words "Behold the man" await our response. Will we choose Jesus or Barabbas?

The second imperative is spoken by the resurrected Christ. According to Luke's Gospel, after appearing to two of the disciples who were traveling on the road to Emmaus (Luke 24:13-35), Jesus then appeared to the whole group of disciples in Jerusalem. Luke records the scene as follows:

> While they were talking about this, Jesus himself stood among them and said to them, "Peace be with you." They were startled and terrified, and thought that they were seeing a ghost. He said to them, "Why are you frightened, and why do doubts arise in your hearts? *Look at my hands and my feet*; see that it is I myself. *Touch me and see*; for a ghost does not have flesh and bones as you see that I have." And when he had said this, *he showed them his hands and his feet*. While in their joy they were disbelieving and still wondering, he said to them, "Have you anything here to eat?" They gave him a piece of broiled fish, and he took it and ate in their presence. (Luke 24:36-43; emphasis added)

Once again the Gospels summon us to look at Jesus, although this time our vantage point must be different. In John's Gospel, we look at Jesus with Pilate and the crowd from a distance—as onlookers. In Luke's account, Jesus stands among his disciples. He and they are one group, not two; they stand with one another, not against. Then, Jesus addresses them in a way that closes any space between them. Jesus invites them not only to look at him and listen to his words but also to touch him. The invitation suggests a tactile proximity to Jesus, as if his disciples may (should?) now place their hands and feet on his, bodying up to him as it were, with such closeness that his wounds are impressed on them. [FIGURE 2.1] Whatever space may be between them now, the disciples no longer have the room to make decisions based on the perspectives of the outsider. Now, when Jesus speaks, his words are so close that their hearts are "startled and terrified" by a presence that is not only seen but also felt. Now, when Jesus says, "touch me," they feel something that causes not only their minds but also their senses to convulse with unruly knowledge: fear mixed with joy; belief mingled with disbelief.

FIGURE 2.1

Eric Gill depicts Mary Magdalene pressing herself against
the crucified Christ. In his personal correspondence, Gill
writes, "I wish I could get you to see the point about Christianity, e.g., when we 'Marry' we don't say to a girl: 'Madam,
you realize that we are the embodiment of an idea.' We say:
'Darling, we two persons are one flesh. It's a love affair first
and last.'" (Cited in R. Griffith-Jones, *Mary Magdalene: The
Woman Whom Jesus Loved* [Norwich, UK: Canterbury Press,
2008], 212.)

Eric Gill. *Nuptials of God*. 1922. Wood engraving on paper. National
Galleries of Scotland. Bequeathed by Sir David Young Cameron 1945.
(Credit: National Galleries of Scotland, used with permission)

I invite you to reflect on the meaning of this second imperative for our Lenten journey. Luke's Gospel suggests that the summons to "behold the man" comes not only to outsiders, like Pilate and the crowd; it comes also to those who profess to be Jesus' disciples, like us. If we locate ourselves among those disciples in Jerusalem, what are we supposed to *see* when Jesus says, "Look at my hands and my feet"? What are we supposed to *feel* when Jesus says, "Touch me and see"? As we think on these questions, I add one more. If, after having seen and touched the hands and feet of the resurrected Christ, we were then to hear him ask us, "Have you anything to eat?"—that is, "Have you anything you can give me that will sustain me for the journey ahead?"—how would we respond? What would we offer as nourishment to one whose hands and feet have experienced what Jesus' have?

I. LUKE'S PORTRAIT OF JESUS' COMPASSION

Each of the Gospels presents a different portrait of Jesus, and these portraits emphasize different aspects of what it means to be a disciple of Jesus. Alan Culpepper accents the differences: "The Markan Jesus is an enigmatic and tragic figure, misunderstood and abandoned. Being a disciple of the Markan Jesus means taking up the cross and following him. The Matthean Jesus is a new Moses who fulfills the Scripture and establishes the authority with his own words. Being a disciple of the Matthean Jesus, therefore, means keeping his teachings and making other disciples."[37] John's Gospel, as we saw in the first presentation, presents Jesus against a cosmic background. "Full of grace and truth" (John 1:14), Jesus comes to redeem not just Bethlehem or Jerusalem, not just Jews or Gentiles of the first century, but the whole world. Being a disciple of John's Jesus means knowing that when Pilate says, "Behold the man," his words place the whole world on trial. How we respond to what we see and understand, John says, has a ripple effect. Beginning with us, the choice for or against Jesus impacts political power, civil and religious institutions, kings, rulers, and all people throughout the world.

---

37. A. Culpepper, "The Gospel of Luke," *NIB*, vol. 9 (Nashville: Abingdon, 1995), 3–4.

Luke's Gospel accents Jesus' compassion. We cannot be sure why Luke has such a keen interest in Jesus' compassion for those who are broken and bruised, but it is worth noting that tradition identifies Luke not only as a companion of Paul but also as a "beloved physician" (cf. Col 4:14; 2 Tim 4:11).[38] Eusebius (fourth century), for example, understands Luke to be one who had expertise in the "art of curing souls." In any case, Luke is more precise than other Gospel writers in his descriptions of the illnesses and afflictions that rob healthy people of life and reduce them to outcasts in a world that readily assumes all suffering is a punishment for sin. In his view, Jesus has come into the world precisely to care for such people. To each and every one, Luke presents the child born in a manger, where vulnerable creatures come for food and refuge, as a Savior come to seek and save the lost (19:10): "To you is born this day in the city of David a Savior, who is the Messiah, the Lord" (2:11).

Toward this end, Luke focuses on the radical inclusiveness of Jesus' ministry, especially to sinners, Samaritans, tax collectors, women, the poor, and the afflicted. Persons who fall into these categories, for whatever reasons, are typically victimized by the regnant social and religious prejudices that define insiders and outsiders. Those who would be Jesus' disciples, Luke says, must learn that these prejudices are wrong; they must be addressed and eliminated. Jesus himself is the model for how to live in the midst of those who suffer. To follow Luke's story is to know that discipleship is seldom easy and almost always costly.

• To the consternation of the religious leaders, Jesus "welcomes sinners and eats with them" (Luke 15:1-2), including tax collectors (5:27-32 [Levi]; 19:1-10 [Zacchaeus]; cf. 18:9-14]), immoral women (7:36-50), and others whose reputations place them beneath society's concern. For this, his critics condemn him by saying, "the Son of Man has come eating and drinking . . . 'Look, a glutton and drunkard, a friend of tax collectors'" (7:34).

---

38. For discussion and visuals, see H. Hornik and M. C. Parsons, *Illuminating Luke: The Infancy Narrative in Italian Renaissance Painting* (New York: Trinity Press International, 2003), 11–28.

• To the consternation of his fellow Jews, who regard the Samaritans as unclean half-breeds, Jesus rebukes them when they want to call down fire on a Samaritan village that refuses to show hospitality to Jews who have long abused them (9:51-56). He tells a parable about a "good Samaritan" whose compassion for the afflicted models the behavior Jesus expects of them (10:29-37). When Jesus goes about his Father's business by healing ten lepers (17:11-19), people who are required to live outside the city and cry out "Unclean, unclean!" (cf. Lev 13:45-46), only one of them, a Samaritan, returns to give praise and thanks for the miracle. To him, Jesus says, "Go on your way; your faith has made you well" (17:19).

• Jesus ministers to both the poor and the rich. Jesus does not withhold compassion from those whose wealth and position might identify them with the oppressive Romans who make life so miserable for the Jews. He heals the Roman centurion's servant (7:1-10) *and* a widow's son (7:11-17). He drives out the demons that afflict a Gentile who lives among the tombs in the country of the Gerasenes (8:26-39), *and* he heals the daughter of Jairus, the leader of the synagogue (8:40-56). He heals the disciple Peter's mother-in-law (4:31-39), *and* a woman from the crowd who has a hemorrhage (8:43-48), *and* a crippled woman who cannot stand up straight (13:10-17). He praises the poor widow who can give but two coins (21:1-4), *but* he rebukes both the rich fool who thinks life consists only of possessions (12:13-21) and the rich man who can't spare even one coin to care for the poor man Lazarus who lies at his gate (16:19-31).

• Pain and suffering are no respecters of persons, Jesus taught, and so neither must be the compassion that comforts and heals them. It is little wonder that when Jesus was invited to table, he insisted that his hosts go out into the streets and find "the poor, the crippled, the lame, and the blind" (14:13, 21), for these are the ones Jesus wants to break bread with.

Such is the way Jesus lived. Such is also the way he died. From Luke's perspective, Jesus "was counted among the lawless" (23:37), and he died with criminals (23:33). And who were those who did the reckoning and looked on the death of this innocent man, whose only crime was compassion for the needy? They were chief priests and religious leaders who were afraid of what Jesus embodied; they were government people who were simply doing their job; they were disciples who saw but couldn't understand. As we turn now to one of Luke's stories about what Jesus requires of those who would be his disciples, the words of Shakespeare's King Lear invite our reflection: "If thou wilt weep my fortune, take my eyes" (IV, 6).

II. ON THE ROAD TO EMMAUS . . . AND BACK (LUKE 24:13-53)

Luke's Gospel begins and ends in Jerusalem, the political and religious center of the Jewish world. The penultimate stop on the journey for Jesus and his disciples, however, is in a little off-the-beaten-track place called Emmaus, northwest of Jerusalem. Luke tells the story of the journey to Emmaus this way.

It had been three days since the disciples had all been in Jerusalem—just a *short* time on the calendar but such a *long* journey for the heart and the mind. They had celebrated the Passover meal with him. They had watched him pray at Gethsemane, at least until he found them "sleeping because of grief," as Luke so tenderly puts it (22:45). They had watched him die at Golgotha, although they stood at a distance for fear someone might recognize them (23:49). They had seen the tomb where Joseph of Arimathea buried him. Now it was the first day of a new week; it was to be their first try at life on the other side of death. It was, we might say today, the first day of the rest of their lives. What were they to do now? How were they to live now that the one they had followed lay dead in a "rock-hewn tomb where no one had ever been laid before" (23:53)?

So it was, Luke tells us, that they came to the tomb at early dawn on the first day of this new week. When they arrived, they saw that the stone had been rolled away. Two men in dazzling clothes told them that Jesus was not there. "He has risen," the men said. Mary Magdalene, Mary the mother of Jesus, and Joanna ran to tell the others, but the others could not believe the news. It seemed to them "an idle tale"; it sounded like nonsense. Even Peter, who had to look for himself, could not believe what he saw. He saw the linen clothes, he found no body, and he went home "amazed at what had happened" (24:12).

Later that same day, two of the disciples were going to Emmaus, a small village about seven miles northwest of Jerusalem. It was an ordinary place, a place that held no particular attraction, a place that promised nothing special. Its precise location on the map is uncertain, although the proposed sites lie along a road that runs generally northwest from Jerusalem. Wherever it may be on the map, Emmaus likely represented a place the disciples headed toward in the hope of getting away from the horrible events they had witnessed in Jerusalem. Frederick Buechner describes such a place this way:

> The place we go in order to escape—a bar, a movie, wherever it is we throw up our hands and say, "Let the whole damned thing go hang. It makes no difference anyway." . . . Emmaus may be buying a new suit or a new car or smoking more cigarettes than you really want, or reading a second-rate novel or even writing one. Emmaus may be going to church on Sunday. Emmaus is whatever we do or wherever we go to make ourselves forget that the world holds nothing sacred: that even the wisest and bravest and loveliest decay and die; that even the noblest ideas that men have had—ideas about love and freedom and justice—have always in time been twisted out of shape by selfish men for selfish ends.[39]

Whatever the reason, they went to Emmaus, and on the way they were talking about all the things that had happened over the last three days. In the midst of their conversations Jesus appeared, but they did not recognize him. "What are you talking about?" Jesus asked them. They simply stared at him, too sad at first to respond. Finally, one named Cleopas answered him: "Are you the only one in Jerusalem who does not know what has happened?" (24:18). Jesus was of course the only one who *did know* what had happened, but they could not yet know this. They were under the impression that they knew more about what had happened than this Jesus who spoke to them from the other side of death. So they journeyed on toward Emmaus, talking to this stranger, telling him *their version* of the story.

In their version (vv. 19-24), they told about the Jesus "of Nazareth" they had known and followed. *They* had known him to be a

---

39. F. Buechner, *The Magnificent Defeat* (New York: Seabury, 1966), 85–86; cf. Culpepper, "Gospel of Luke," 482.

"prophet mighty in deed and word before God," but "*all [the rest of]* *the people*" had refused to accept him and had handed him over to be crucified. They conveniently overlooked or tried to forget their own complicity in calling for Jesus' death (23:18-21). In their minds, they were guilty of nothing more than misplaced trust: "We had hoped that he was the one to redeem Israel," but now he was dead. This "stranger" Jesus who was listening to their story responded by asking them what Scripture said about prophets. Did not Scripture say, "beginning with Moses and all the prophets," that it was necessary for the Messiah to suffer? That "suffering," even unto death, was part of God's chosen plan for all those who would follow the Messiah and "enter into his glory"? Still, the two disciples were convinced they had been wrong—about Scripture, about Jesus, about God, about their discipleship—and so they journeyed on, disappointed, sad, confused.

When they came close to the village, this stranger walked on ahead, as if he was preparing to leave them behind. They urged him to stay. It was almost evening, and at least he could stay long enough to share a meal with them. Jesus agreed, and they gathered around the table. Then something truly miraculous happened. Jesus took some bread, blessed it, broke it in two, and gave it to them. Suddenly they were back at the Passover table, where they had shared their last meal with him three days ago. Now "their eyes were opened, and they recognized him" (24:31). And then, just as suddenly, he vanished.

In telling his story, Luke does not so much as pause here, but perhaps we should, for this is a dramatic and revelatory moment. It is akin to the tradition in Greco-Roman literature of entertaining "angels unawares," a tradition that also connects with Scripture, perhaps most explicitly in Hebrews 13:2: "Do not neglect to show hospitality to strangers, for by doing that some have entertained angels without knowing it" (NRSV).[40] Artists have certainly been captured by Luke's account of "the supper at Emmaus," and their exegesis of the scene helps us understand what the disciples may have

---

40. The allusion is most likely to Abraham and Sarah's welcoming of three visitors who brought the good news of a promised son (Gen 18:1-21), but there are several other stories of hospitality to mysterious strangers that contribute to the tradition (cf. Gen 19:1-14; Judg 6:11-18; 13:3-22; Tob 12:1-20).

seen and recognized at this pregnant moment in Emmaus, a place where, as Buechner puts it, the world seems to hold nothing sacred.

Rembrandt is representative of many artists who center their attention on the beatific Christ at table with his disciples. Framed by a shimmering light that radiates divinity, Jesus is portrayed as one whose identity stands in such marked contrast to those around him that we wonder how anyone could fail to understand who he is.[41] [FIGURE 2.2]

FIGURE 2.2

Rembrandt (1606-1669). *The Supper at Emmaus.* 1648. Oil on wood. Louvre, Paris. (Credit: Wikimedia Commons, PD-US)

41. See further, J. I Durham, *The Biblical Rembrandt: Human Painter in a Landscape of Faith* (Macon, GA: Mercer University Press, 2004).

Other artists have exegeted the scene differently. I am particularly struck by the contrast between two paintings by the Italian
artist Caravaggio (1571–1610).[42] In his 1602 painting of the supper,
Caravaggio also uses light to illumine what he sees to be central in
Luke's account. [FIGURE 2.3] And here too the light draws our
attention to Christ, especially to his face—youthful, sensual, beard-
less, and framed by flowing hair. Christ's hands, smooth and delicate,
extend in a sacramental gesture of blessing the host. Our sense is that
Christ is truly a vision of God. The disciples at table with him are
painted and posed differently. Their faces are rugged and bearded,
they are clothed in torn working dress, and their heavy fishermen's

FIGURE 2.3

Caravaggio (1571–1610). *Supper at Emmaus*. 1602. Oil on canvas.
National Gallery, London. (Credit: Wikimedia Commons, PD-US)

---

42. For the following discernments concerning the connections between Cara-
vaggio's life and his paintings, I draw on H. Langdon, *Caravaggio: A Life* (New
York: Farrar, Straus and Giroux, 1998). For close attention to Caravaggio and
Luke's passion narratives, see H. J. Hornik and M. C. Parsons, *Illuminating Luke:
The Passion and Resurrection Narratives in Italian Renaissance and Baroque Painting*,
vol. 3 (New York: T & T Clark, 2008), 118–49.

hands display different gestures. Cleopas thrusts back his chair and the other disciple stretches out his arms, both gestures that suggest a flurry of action in response to the tranquil blessing that is going on in their midst. Both disciples are further distinguished from the stocky innkeeper, who is standing in dark shadows with his hands in his belt, "a brilliant gesture of blunt incomprehension."[43]

But Caravaggio also uses the light to show that in the midst of all that is so clearly divine, there is much that remains very earthy, very life-like, very ordinary, as if to suggest that the holy is always present and available in the reality of the everyday world, if we but have eyes to see. The scene is set in a Roman tavern, with rough wooden chairs; the one that Cleopas pushes backwards seems so close to us, the onlookers, that we are about to be brought into the picture. The light falls across an assortment of ordinary items arranged on a cloth-covered table: a glazed jug, a half-filled pitcher, loaves of bread, a platter of fish (presumably), and a bowl of lush, ripened local fruits balanced precariously on the table's edge, as if at any moment it too will fall toward us. Should we reach out to steady it in its place or take it and eat from it ourselves?

What Caravaggio offers us is no doubt informed by his own situation in life. His own reality shaped the way he read the Lukan text and the way he saw the Lukan Christ. He painted *Supper at Emmaus* sometime around 1600–1601, when he was thirty years old. At the time, he was at the height of his public success. During 1601, and probably until 1602 or 1603, he stayed in the Palazzo Mattei, the splendid home of Cardinal Girolamo Mattei, the head of a Roman family of venerated antiquity who served as his patrons and benefactors. During this period, Caravaggio painted a number of outstanding gallery paintings, including *St. John the Baptist*, *The Taking of Christ*, and *Doubting Thomas*. He was paid handsomely for each. For the *Supper at Emmaus*, for example, he received 150 scudi (gold and silver coins).

Three years later, Caravaggio returned to the story of the supper at Emmaus. [FIGURE 2.4] Once again he uses a combination of light and shadows to exegete the Lukan text. The scene is similar to the earlier painting, but there are striking differences. Where the

---

43. Langdon, *Caravaggio*, 231.

FIGURE 2.4

Caravaggio (1571–1610). *Supper at Emmaus.* 1605. Oil on canvas. Brera Art Gallery, Milan. (Credit: Wikimedia Commons, PD–US)

previous painting shines the light on a beatific Christ, this frailer, bearded Christ almost vanishes into shadows. There remains a sacramental gravity in the way he gestures toward the meal before them—bread not broken, a single jug of wine, a rack of lamb, suggestive of the sacrificed lamb of God that requires one to taste death in order to live, and an inn table now covered by a carpet that makes it look more like an altar. The bowl of ripened and inviting fruit is no longer present. The scene is not painted in the bright colors of the previous work but instead in duller browns and grays, as if to suggest that none of the persons at table with Jesus can be clearly differentiated from the dark shadows that hover all around. With the left side of his face receding into the shadows, Jesus himself is half-hidden.

This too, Caravaggio suggests, is Emmaus, but seen differently. This too is a moment of revelation, but it conveys more weariness than energy. What seems to be foremost in Caravaggio's mind is not Luke 24:32, the moment of realization when the disciples' eyes were opened to the reality before them and they exclaimed, "Did not our hearts burn within us . . . ?" Instead, he seems to be pondering an earlier moment in Luke 24:29, when at the end of a weary day of traveling the disciples say to Jesus, "Stay with us, please, for it is almost evening and the day is now nearly over."[44] There is the offer of sacrament here, but it is shrouded in darkness, and the postures of those at table with Jesus invite us to wonder whether they are leaning in because they see it or because they don't.

We have here two pictures of the same supper at Emmaus, both connected to reality but a reality seen from different vantage points. We are reminded once more that Caravaggio painted out of the reality of his own life. In the earlier painting, he was in his prime, respected, sought after, wealthy, secure. By the time he painted the second version of the *Supper at Emmaus*, his world had changed dramatically. In the years 1603–1606, Rome was under siege. Relations between the governing families and the Church were in turmoil. The atmosphere in which religious artists like Caravaggio worked became repressive, especially so when Cardinal Vicario (1603) renewed an edict setting forth stringent guidelines for religious art, including the requirement that painters who failed to obtain a license for their work should be fined twenty-five scudi, or suffer imprisonment, exile, or even greater punishments.[45] In the midst of these shifting political winds, Caravaggio's personal life began to unravel. He was sued for libel, imprisoned for a time for his role in an act of street violence, and then, while trying to extricate himself from a fight with a longtime enemy named Ranuccio Tomassoni, he drew his sword, stabbed him in the stomach, and killed him. For about a month nothing happened, but once investigations were made and the publicity concerning the killing raised the profile of the case, Caravaggio was charged with murder and (apparently) sentenced to die. He fled Rome to save himself and spent the rest of his life (1605–1610) sick and impoverished, banished in exile in Malta, Naples, and Sicily. He eventually received a pardon from the Pope only to die in mysterious circumstances on the way back to Rome in 1610.

Caravaggio's second version of the supper at Emmaus was painted in 1605, when he had fled Rome as a man condemned to die. He

---

44. Ibid., 316.
45. Ibid., 275.

had killed a man, and his first instinct as a good Catholic, we may assume, was to make an act of contrition in the hope of obtaining forgiveness.[46] It is in such a world as this that the colors of this 1605 version of Emmaus go from bright to dull, that the light becomes muted by shadows, that the promise of the sacrament seems wearily out of reach for a person like him. As Luke's Gospel puts it, the day is far spent, night is falling, and the journey that lies ahead, if indeed there is still a journey to be made, seems to have dead-ended in despair.

With these two visual images of the meal at Emmaus in our mind's eye, we resume Luke's story where we left off, at v. 30: "While he was at the table with them, he took bread, blessed and broke it, and gave it to them. Then their eyes were opened, and they recognized him, and he vanished from their sight." Luke continues the story by reporting that once the disciples recognized Jesus, their hearts burned within them. Now they sensed that they understood everything he had taught them before he died. Luke says that at that very hour they got up and returned to Jerusalem. They found the rest of the disciples and told them what had happened on the road to Emmaus, how Jesus had made himself known to them in the breaking of the bread. Now they were all ready to share in the post-resurrection Hallelujah that we too have heard and proclaimed as our own: "The Lord has risen indeed!" (24:35).

"Hallelujah. The Lord has risen indeed." It seems like just the right ending for the story. They thought Jesus was dead; now they knew he was alive. They had not recognized him at first; now their eyes were opened, and they saw him. They had been sad over their loss; now their hearts burned with a newfound fervor. They had left the holy city on a journey to nowhere; now they were back in Jerusalem, ready to spread the good news far and wide. They seem to be at the same place we will be on Easter morning, when we gather with Christians round the world to sing and celebrate the good news of the resurrection—such a perfect ending to the story. And so we prime ourselves to respond to their affirmation: "Hallelujah, Christ is risen. He is risen indeed!"

---

46. Ibid., 316.

This seems like such a good place to end the story that I wonder why Luke does not put a period after verse 35 and close the book on his Gospel. Once the disciples can make the confession that Christ has risen from the grave, what is left to say? What more than this do they need to know? Perhaps the disciples were just as surprised as we are to learn that there is more to the Easter story than the affirmation that Christ is risen. Luke seems to be saying that Easter morning praise, if it is to be authentic, must stretch past Sunday. It must spill into the rest of our lives. If it does not translate into concrete deeds, day by day, that mirror Jesus' compassion for the outcasts— "the poor, the crippled, the lame, and the blind" (Luke 14:13) who must always be welcome at Jesus' table—then it counts for nothing.

The rest of Luke's story about what happened on the other side of that first Easter is recorded in verses 36-53. While the disciples were in Jerusalem, still talking about these things, presumably while the words "The Lord has risen indeed" were still ringing in the air, Luke reports that Jesus came and stood in their presence one more time. He greeted them with familiar words that should have put them at ease—"Peace be with you"—but they were "startled and terrified." After all they had shared with Jesus on this long day's journey to Emmaus, they could not recognize the one who spoke to them. Just moments before, they had recognized and acclaimed him as the risen Lord; now they think they are seeing a ghost. For the second time this day Jesus does something truly remarkable. He says to all of them, "Look at my hand and my feet . . . . Touch me and see that it is I myself" (24:39). And then, while they are "disbelieving and still wondering" (24:41) what it all means, he asks them if they have any food to offer him. *He* has just given *them* bread, blessed and broken. Now he asks *them* to feed *him*. They give him a piece of fish, the same kind of food they have seen him use to feed the five thousand who followed him into a deserted place outside Bethsaida (Luke 9:10-17). He takes the fish and eats in their presence. Luke pauses just at this point to allow us to take a close look at this scene: Jesus with scarred hands and feet, asking for food; disciples, disbelieving and wondering, offering him the only thing they have.

I am struck by those words, "Look at my hands and feet." Why did Jesus think it important for the disciples to look at his hands and his feet? Commentators usually suggest that Jesus wants to show them that he is not a ghost. He is real; he is tangibly present with them; he is indeed truly alive. Surely this must be part of the reason for what he does. But is there more to it than this? The disciples seem to have already recognized that he is real. When they saw him breaking the bread, they knew he was Jesus, the same one who had shared Passover with them. And had they not already seen his hands and feet? They were at Golgotha. They saw him being crucified. Even though they stood at a safe distance, surely the disciples knew what kind of scars the spikes would leave when they were nailed to their target.

"Look at my hands and feet . . . . Touch me and see." What a strange command for Jesus to give to disciples on that first Easter morning, especially after they clearly already understood enough to shout to the heavens, "The Lord is risen indeed!" Why would Jesus want them to look at his wounds and scars again? What were they supposed to *see* and *feel* on this side of Easter that they didn't see and feel before?

III. LOOKING AT THE DISCIPLES LOOKING AT JESUS

My musings on this question have led to a rereading of Wallace Stegner's novel *Crossing to Safety*. A scene from near the end of the book describes the vacation Sally and her husband take to Italy, along with another couple with whom they have shared years of friendship. They visit the tiny village of Sansepolchro in southern Tuscany. There they happen upon Piero della Francesca's fifteenth century fresco of the resurrected Christ. [FIGURE 2.5] On the left, the painting depicts a barren landscape with naked trees reaching toward a darkening sky. To the right, the landscape is alive with foliage, human dwellings, and bursts of sunlight. Between these scenes of life and death, della Francesca places the resurrected Christ, with one foot still in the tomb as if he is still in the act of stepping out of the grave. In Christ's right hand is a staff holding a flag of victory. On his left hand and foot we can see the crucifixion scars. His side shows the wound from the soldier's spear, still dripping blood.[47]

---

47. See further F. Dabell, J. V. Field, "Piero della Francesca," *Oxford Art Online* (Oxford: Oxford University Press), oxfordartonline.com/benezit/abstract/

FIGURE 2.5

Piero della Francesca (1415–1492). *The Resurrection.* c. 1462–1464. Mural
in fresco and tempera. Museo Civico di Sansepolcro. (Credit: Wikimedia
Commons, PD–US)

Sally's husband and their friends stop casually to look at the
painting, as tourists often do, and then they move on. Sally lingers
behind. She is fixed on the face of Francesca's Christ. [FIGURE 2.6]
Despite the golden halo over Christ's head and the flag of victory in

10.1093/benz/9780199773787.001.0001/acref-9780199773787-e-00141439;
J. R. Banker, *Piero della Francesca: Artist and Man* (Oxford: Oxford University
Press, 2014), 107–13; H. J. Hornik, *The Art of Christian Reflection* (Waco: Baylor
University Press, 2018), 173–75.

FIGURE 2.6

Piero della Francesca. Detail of *The Resurrection*. c. 1462–1464. Mural in fresco and tempera. Museo Civico di Sansepolcro. (Credit: Wikimedia Commons, PD-US)

his hand, she notices that his eyes are staring into the foreground with a look that seems to be remembering the pain of crucifixion, as if to suggest that "if resurrection had taken place, it had not yet been comprehended."[48] Sally's husband notices her staring at the painting. He wonders what has so captured her interest and imagination. He looks at her intently. She is standing there, propped up on the crutches she has needed to walk since a childhood bout with polio crippled her with a lasting lesson about what pain and loss means. His eyes return to the painting and then again to Sally, and, gradually but with increasing clarity, he understands what Sally sees in the eyes of this one who until moments ago had been horribly dead. The truth and the promise of resurrection, he now sees, is that "those who

48. W. Stegner, *Crossing to Safety* (New York: Random House, 1987), 221.

have been dead understand things that will never be understood by those who have only lived."[49]

"Those who have been dead understand things that will never be understood by those who have only lived." I wonder, could it be that what Sally saw in this painting is what Luke suggests the Christ, who is ever defined by compassion for the broken and the bruised, wants every disciple to see on this side of Easter? "Look at my hands and feet . . . . Touch me and see." Could it be that on this side of the empty tomb we are supposed to know more about pain and suffering, more about hurt and brokenness than we did three days ago? Could it be that we need to look again at his wounded hands and his feet, look again at those eyes that teach us what it means to hang on a cross of affliction, suspended between darkness and despair? Could it be that we are not ready to shout the good news of life everlasting until we have learned to listen to the screams of those who like Jesus are trapped in a world that seems to be empty of God? "Look at my hands and feet . . . . Touch me and see."

In his novel *A Place on Earth*, Wendell Berry gives us a picture of what it means to bring good news to those who live in a world of hurt and brokenness. The central family in the story is the Feltners. Their only son Virgil is a war casualty. He has been "missing in action" so long that the family must now admit to themselves that Virgil is dead. Into this scene of death and loss comes Brother Preston, the family's minister. Upon his arrival, the Feltners dry up their tears and listen for the word from God that might speak to their hurt.

Brother Preston talks to them about heavenly things, truths about the "Hereafter," the promise of eternal life. But his words seem oddly disconnected from the grief that gnaws away at their insides. They listen, patiently and respectfully, until the minister has his say. When he finishes, he excuses himself and returns to the church to prepare for Sunday's sermon.

After the pastor has gone, the Feltners resume their crying. Mat, the father, reflects on the gap between the words of heavenly hope that Brother Preston has offered and the hurt they feel so deeply that they cannot hear. He comes to this conclusion: "In the preacher's words the Heavenly City has risen up, surmounting [our] lives,

---

49. Ibid., 222.

the house, the town—the final hope, in which all the riddles and ends of the world are gathered, illuminated, and bound." But then Mat continues, "This is the preacher's hope, and he has moved to it alone, *outside the claims of time and sorrow*."[50] Death has taught the Feltners a hard lesson, a lesson they could not have learned from life alone: words that come from "outside the claims of time and sorrow" cannot connect those who suffer to God. Only those who know what it means to live *inside the claims of time and sorrow* can speak words that make sense to the Feltners.

Friends, somewhere out there, as we make this Lenten journey together, there is a person named Feltner who is crying. Perhaps they live across the street or on the other side of the tracks; perhaps it is the person with whom we work; perhaps it is someone in our family; perhaps it is someone we know; perhaps it is someone we will meet tomorrow. Perhaps the one who is crying is not out there. Perhaps it is someone sitting in the seat beside us. Maybe the person named Feltner is you. Their cry—your cry—may sound like the one we remembered in the first presentation: "My God, my God why have you forsaken me?" Their cry—your cry—may sound like the ones we read about in today's newspaper; perhaps it is like those anguished cries piercing the heavens from the refugees in Albania, Macedonia, Montenegro. Whoever they are and wherever they are, people like the Feltners are crying for help. They desperately need some word from God that will make a difference in a world where sorrow has staked out its claim on life. Who can say or do anything that will help?

Brother Preston was supposed to be an agent of God's compassion, but he did not have the words. He knew all about the "*hereafter*," but he did not understand what it means to live in *the here and now*, on this side of this grave, where death teaches things that are deeper than life. The disciples on the road to Emmaus had seen Jesus; they had recognized him, broken bread with him, acclaimed him with what they thought was an Easter faith: "The Lord has risen indeed!" And yet while they were still full and flush with the energy of this very acclamation, Jesus came to them one more time. "Look at my hands and feet . . . . Touch me and see." "Look . . . touch . . . see."

---

50. W. Berry, *A Place on Earth* (San Francisco: North Point, 1983), 94.

And after he showed them his hands and feet, he said to them, "Have you anything here to eat?" Only then were they able to give him the fish that once before he had blessed and broken and given to those who hungered for sustenance in a "deserted place." Jesus seems to be teaching his disciples that on the other side of death, they—we—are supposed to know more about pain and suffering than before. And they—we—*are supposed to live inside the claims of this hurt.* If we do not, it is likely that all the Feltners of this world will still be crying for help long after we have gone back to church.

According to Luke's Gospel, after Jesus had showed them his hands and feet, he led them back out of Jerusalem (24:50-53). They stopped at Bethany, where he had lifted up his hands and blessed them. Bethany was the town located just outside Jerusalem on the eastern slopes of the Mount of Olives. It was the last station for the pilgrim traveling from Jordan to Jerusalem; the place where Lazarus was raised from the grave; the place where Jesus was anointed in the house of Simon the leper (Mark 14:3-9; Matt 26:6-13). Bethany was the place where Jesus had spent his last week of ministry before heading into Jerusalem. It was from Bethany that the disciples got the donkey that Jesus rode into the last days of his life on earth.

Jesus took them back to Bethany, back to where their journey towards Easter began. They had already passed to the other side of the empty tomb; they already knew how to proclaim the Easter message. But Jesus took them back for one more look at how the road to life always passes through death. While he was blessing them, he withdrew from them and ascended into heaven. Luke suggests that the last thing they saw of Jesus were his nail-marked hands and feet, extended in blessing. Then they returned to Jerusalem again. Now they were filled with great joy. Now they were ready to begin their own ministry by offering the blessing of God. Now they knew that the world is full of affliction that can only be comforted by those who have looked closely at Jesus' hands and feet. Now they know more than they did before about what it means to hang suspended inside the claims of time and sorrow, with one hand touching *him* and the other blessing *them*, all the Feltners of this world, in his name.

This is the gospel lesson for the first Sunday after Easter. What then shall we say to these things? When Paul tried to teach the early church the truth about Jesus' life, death, and resurrection, he put it this way:

> Do you not know that all of us who have been baptized into Christ Jesus were *baptized into his death*? Therefore we have been *buried with him by baptism into death*, so that, just as Christ was raised from the dead by the glory of God, so we too might walk in newness of life. For *if we have been united with him in a death like his*, we will certainly be united with him in a resurrection like his. (Rom 6:3-5)

We have been buried, blessed, and united in death. Let us go forth into this Lenten journey knowing that its claim on us extends well past Easter Sunday's "Hallelujah!" Why? Because if we have eyes to see, someone right around the corner is about to ask us a question: "Do you have anything to eat?" Jesus expects his disciples, all of those who have touched and seen what suffering means, to be able to set a table and say, "Yes, I do."

3

Regarding the Pain of Others

Our Lenten journey towards the empty tomb goes through Golgotha, where three men hang on wooden crosses. One of them is innocent of the charges brought against him. The other two have apparently been justly charged. Whatever the evidence of their crimes, each one has been found guilty. Each one is dead.

Thus far, we have viewed what has happened from two perspectives. First, we stood with the crowd in John 19, outside Pilate's headquarters, and we looked on as he presented the "King of the Jews." The honor the title suggests seemed lost in the way Jesus appeared before us. His crown was made of thorns; his royal robes were torn and bloodstained, barely covering the welt marks on his body; his beard dripped with the spit of mockery. Pilate handed him over to the crowd. The crowd around us yelled out, "Crucify him! Crucify him!" and then handed him over to the executioners. We heard Pilate's words, "Behold the man"; we looked at Pilate, and we looked at the crowd looking at this one named Jesus, and we wondered, what are we supposed to see, what are we supposed to do? After all, we are only onlookers.

Next, we walked with the disciples on the road from Jerusalem to Emmaus and back again (Luke 24). We felt like one of them, like insiders, like those who belong in the inner circle. We were close enough to see their sadness and confusion; close enough to see their surprise upon encountering a stranger who did not know about the tragedy they had experienced; close enough to hear the conversation between them, to see the stranger break bread, bless it, and give it to them. We were close enough to see their eyes open wide with recognition; close enough to feel the energy in their run back to Jerusalem to tell the others, to sense the excitement when they all agreed, "The Lord has risen indeed!" And we were close enough to be "startled and terrified" when the risen Lord suddenly appeared again and said, "Look at my hands and feet . . . . Touch me and see." We heard the words. We looked at the disciples looking at Jesus, who was looking at us as if the words were addressed to us as well, and we wondered: what are we supposed to see in those hands and feet? If we touch those hands and feet, what are we supposed to feel? After all, even insiders sometimes feel like strangers in their own crowd.

My purpose in inviting you to look from two perspectives at this journey we make with Jesus is to suggest that outsiders and insiders often see the same thing differently. Pilate does not see Jesus in the same way the disciples do. How we regard the suffering of another depends on where we stand, whether we are on the outside looking in or on the inside looking at things more closely. I suspect that on first thought, each of us would probably agree that closer is better. When it comes to the choice of standing with Pilate or with the disciples, who among us would say we prefer to stand with Pilate because he sees things more knowingly? But even as we take our stand with the insiders, perhaps all too confidently, we may flinch at the memory of Jesus' parable concerning those "who trusted in themselves that *they* were righteous and regarded *others* with contempt" (Luke 18:9). Luke tells the story as follows:

> Two men went up to the temple to pray, one a Pharisee [read: religious insider] and the other a tax collector [read: religious outsider]. The Pharisee, standing by himself, was praying thus, "God, I thank you that I am not like *other people*: thieves, rogues, adulterers, or even like this tax collector. I fast twice a week; I give a tenth of all my income." But the tax collector, *standing far off*, would not even look up to heaven, but was beating his breast and saying, "God, be merciful to me, a sinner!"

And then Jesus' verdict, which may cause all of us who are tempted to regard "the others with contempt" to shudder:

> I tell you, this man [the one "standing far off"] went down to his home justified rather than the other; for all who exalt themselves will be humbled, but all who humble themselves will be exalted. (Luke 18:10-14)

In truth, the distinction between insiders and outsiders blurs. The difference is never as clear as we may think or want. As he ponders what to do with Jesus, Pilate, the outsider, moves back and forth. Inside his headquarters, he sees that Jesus is innocent. Outside, he sees that the crowd and politics require that Jesus be found guilty. When he hands Jesus over to be executed, he does so as a *conflicted outsider*. The disciples are un-conflicted insiders. They are members of the inner circle, the ones privileged to share table fellowship with Jesus. So when their master and friend breaks bread with them and then says, "one of you will betray me . . . , and his hand is on the table" (Matt 26:21; Luke 22:21), they cannot believe that Jesus could be referring to any one of them. And yet, three short days later, when Jesus appears in their midst, they do not recognize him. He is like a stranger in their presence, *until* they see his wounded hands and feet and feel his pain up close. In the end, they are *conflicted insiders*. When it comes to looking at Jesus, the disciples are not that different from Pilate. They are all conflicted; they are all both "disbelieving and wondering" (Luke 24:41).

Since this is the third of five presentations, perhaps it is time to lay my cards on the table. In every good pentad, as I keep reminding my students, it is the third or middle item that provides the all-important hinge on which everything else hangs. In the Pentateuch, for example, as I take great delight in pointing out to my students, it is the third book, the book of Leviticus, that anchors the whole; without it, nothing else in the Torah really makes sense. So here is my thesis: How we "regard" another person's pain and suffering depends, in large measure, on *perspective*. I suggest that we define perspective in *relational terms*. That is, perspective has to do with more than just being an outsider or an insider. Both outsiders and insiders can watch what is going on, but watching, even up close, is still just watching.

Something more is required. Simply put, the eye is connected with the brain, and the brain is connected with the nervous system.[51]

If the information the eye sees goes to the brain but no further, then it produces knowledge that remains primarily cognitive. We *think* about what we have seen. Thinking is a good thing, for how else could we process and make sense of all the information that floods our minds? When we look on someone else's pain, we may stand back and *think through* the situation until we come to some important principle that is at stake; we may think about the justice or injustice of this one's fortunes. There is nothing wrong with standing back and thinking about we have learned by looking at things from a distance. But *thinking is not feeling*. There is a safe space between the two that allows us to be abstract, not personal; we theorize about suffering without wincing from its pain. That might be enough, were the brain not connected to the nervous system. It is the nervous system that requires us to respond to the stimuli of knowledge. It is one thing to know that fire will burn us; it is quite another to feel the pain of the flame and respond by moving our hand away. My thesis, in other words, is this: When Jesus says to those who would be his disciples, "Look at my hands and my feet . . . . *Touch* me and see," he hopes and expects that they will respond with something more than a cogent theory about pain and suffering. Touching the hands and feet of someone who has been bloodied and bruised by suffering triggers our nervous system to act, to do something because we have felt something. Thus, the title for this presentation—"Regarding the Pain of Others"—invites at least one more question: When we "touch and see" the pain of another, *what do we do?*

I. *REGARDING THE PAIN OF OTHERS.* WHAT SHOULD WE LEARN? WHAT SHOULD WE DO?

The genesis of this presentation, indeed of all five of these presentations, is Susan Sontag's book *Regarding the Pain of Others*. She introduces the book by citing Virginia Woolf's reflections on the fascist insurrection in Spain in *Three Guineas*, published in 1938. An eminent lawyer in London had written to Woolf asking, "How in

---

51. I adapt the insight from Susan Sontag (*Regarding the Pain of Others*, 26), who borrows it from Virginia Woolf.

your opinion are we to prevent war?" Woolf responded with a denun-
ciation of war that echoed many others of the time, including those
of the lawyer himself. Referring to the photographic images of war
that were constantly being published in the newspapers at the time—
pictures of bombed-out houses and horribly mangled dead bodies
strewn across the ground—Woolf assumed that the pictures could
only unite people of good will in common revulsion. Why? Because
we are not monsters or barbarians. We are educated people who can
think and feel and act appropriately; of course, we recoil at images
of brutality inflicted on others. As Woolf says to the lawyer, "*We* are
seeing with you the same dead bodies, the same ruined houses."[52]

Woolf's use of the word "we" gives Sontag pause. Do *we* all really
see the same thing, react the same way, when we look on the suffering
of others? After all, if *we* all were truly convulsed by the horrible
pain caused by war, would there not be such a widespread conviction
that war is definitionally evil, that its cost so far outweighs its gain
that we would never, under any circumstances, lend our support to
those who seek to wage war against others? If we were all truly of one
accord in seeing war as abhorrent, then peace would be the norm.
This, of course, is not the history of the world we know. When we
examine the facts coldly, we are forced to admit that war has been the
norm; peace has been the exception. Sontag introduces her quandary
on thinking about Woolf's response to the lawyer with an observation that set me to thinking about what I might say as we embark on
the Lenten journey together: "No 'we' should be taken for granted
when the subject is looking at other people's pain."[53]

Sontag's book is short in terms of pages (126), a relatively quick
read, but it is long on important ideas, and I cannot do it justice
here. In the hope that a picture may really be worth a thousand
words, let me show you the picture she uses on the dustjacket of her
book. [FIGURE 3.1] Francisco de Goya (1746–1828) was one of the
triumvirate of great Spanish masters, along with El Greco and Diego
Velázquez. El Greco expressed the spirituality of Spain. Velázquez
conveyed the elegance of the Spanish society in which he lived. Goya,
who by the end of his career had contracted a serious disease that

---

52. Sontag, *Regarding the Pain of Others*, 6 (emphasis added).
53. Ibid., 7.

FIGURE 3.1

Francisco de Goya (1746–1828). Plate 36, "Not this!" *The Disasters of War*. 1810–1820. Etching with aquatint. Museum of Fine Arts, Houston, Texas. (Credit: Wikimedia Commons, PD-US)

left him totally deaf, was instinctively attuned to the pain of life. His disappointment and rage at humanity's capacity to hurt those regarded as the "enemy" with barbarous, often indifferent, cruelty is nowhere so clearly depicted as in the eighty-two etchings he made between 1810 and 1820, titled *The Disasters of War* (all but three plates were first published in 1863, thirty-five years after his death), in which he depicts the atrocities committed by Napoleon's soldiers, who invaded Spain in 1808 to quell the insurrection against French rule.[54] His objective was to move the viewers close enough to the horror of war to convince them that what they see is more than a spectacle.

In this picture, Goya shows three dead men hanging from trees, suggestively evocative of the three crosses on Golgotha. He

---

54. See further J. Tomlinson, *Goya: A Portrait of the Artist* (Princeton: Princeton University Press, 2020).

foregrounds one of these images, giving us a side view of a dead man, hanging limp from a forked branch of a tree that itself appears to have just enough life to support the added burden. The dead weight tilts the tree and its burden to the right, as if it is just minutes before being finally uprooted, at which point we may imagine both the tree and the body will fall forward into the lap of one of Napoleon's soldiers, who is taking a break from his duties to look on the scene from a distance. The soldier sits in repose; his right arm is crooked, and his right hand is on his waist in a gesture of contemplation. He rests his head in his left hand. His uniform is clean, unstained by the blood of war. He looks on with an indifferent expression.

The literal space between the soldier and the corpse is small, about a half-inch at the bottom between their feet, an inch and a half at the top between their faces. If this were a scene in a film, a moving picture, we could easily imagine that the distance is about to be closed: in the next scene, either the corpse will fall and touch the soldier, or the soldier will move a foot, perhaps rise up, reach out, and touch the man. But the picture freezes time; everything stands still in a wordless, actionless proximity. The space between the two men is small, but at this moment it seems immeasurable, and we viewers are left to contemplate how far it is and what it takes to close the gap between the living and the dead. For the duration of this presentation, I invite you to imagine yourself into this scene, into the soul of this dead man, into the soul of this soldier, and from both of these perspectives to think about the distance that separates them. If there were to be a next scene, what would you want it to show?

II. LOOKING ON THROUGH THE EYES OF THE SOLDIER

We imagine ourselves first into the mind and heart of this soldier. What might he be seeing as he looks on this corpse? What might he be feeling? I imagine three different scenarios.

(1) Perhaps he is thinking that war is hell; it causes enormous pain and suffering, but it is, after all, sometimes a necessary evil. Perhaps he takes comfort in the thought that as a French soldier, he is on the side of right. These rebel insurrectionists are no more than terrorists; if they are not stopped, they will bring down the government and cause violence that is worse than the war that is required

to defeat them. As W. H. Auden once observed, "Violence is never just; though justice may sometimes require it."[55] Auden wrote these words in 1969–1971, not about the Spanish insurrection but rather in the aftermath of the two world wars, Korea, and Vietnam. Still, in the wake of 9/11, "Ground Zero," and our own ongoing war on terrorism, his words might at first seem like a sound bite from one of President Bush's State of the Union addresses. We may not have much sympathy for the Roman soldiers who were only following orders when they executed Jesus for being a subversive; we may not feel much connection with this French soldier who was only following Napoleon's orders; but when it comes to terrorists who fly their planes into our own New York's World Trade Center, it is not hard to rationalize that sometimes justice may indeed require violence.[56]

As we think on these things, two other comments should be added to the mix. Auden completed the words cited above with a second line: "Violence is never just, though justice may sometimes require it: *tyrants are persons to whom requisite evil is fun.*" And Goya, who starts our thinking with this picture, seems also to want to direct us to a specific conclusion. His caption for this picture reads, "Not this [either]!"

(2) Perhaps this soldier is a veteran of too many campaigns, too many wars. Perhaps he has seen too much suffering, so much that he can only make peace with his conscience by forgetting. There is simply too much pain in this world; its scope seems cosmic, too vast, too epic, too irrevocable to be changed. What else can a soldier who has seen too much do but simply take a deep breath and try to get ready for the next assignment? As Sontag notes, when suffering is conceived on so grand a scale, "compassion can only flounder—and

---

55. W. H. Auden, *W. H. Auden: Collected Poems* (New York: Vintage International, 1991), 859.

56. The examples used in the original presentation are time specific (the Vietnam war, 9/11, President George W. Bush), but the larger point remains salient. As I prepare these presentations for publication, the United States along with the world community is in the middle of pandemic triggered by Covid-19. In the midst of a worldwide search for a vaccine, there is an increasing call for retribution against China, the supposed source of the virus.

make abstract."[57] Perhaps the soldier's apparent indifference is nothing more than the price he pays for doing his duty. Like a doctor who has spent a career in the trauma unit, he can only do his job if he remains objective. Too much identification with the patient may compromise his skill.

We might all agree that too much exposure to the pain that is everywhere in this world desensitizes us to its reality. After a while, we see so many pictures that we simply become numb. We look, and then we turn the page, change the channel, or simply walk away and forget. Another suicide bomber has blown up a bus in Jerusalem; another soldier in another war has died; another victim of an unexpected virus has died. Today's headline tragedies are tomorrow's recycled newspapers. There are so many images of pain and suffering, coming at us from so many different directions, that they simply lose their shock value. Whatever moral outrage we might have felt at the beginning is finally reducible to a succinct, if crude, bumper sticker cliché: "Shit happens." Ho-hum.

The evidence that we do all indeed sooner or later yield to the temptation to trivialize the pain of others is all around. Sontag cites a number of examples. I appropriate one of hers and add one of my own for your consideration.

The camera was invented in 1839. By the 1940s, war photography was appearing regularly in newspapers and magazines. In this country, the standard was set early on by *Life* magazine, first published in 1936 (also by the French *Vu*, 1929, and the British *Picture Post*, 1938). In the July 12, 1937, issue, the famed war photographer Robert Capa published a full-page picture of a Republican soldier being shot to death.[58] [FIGURE 3.2] By clicking the shutter with professional expertise, he captured the expression on the victim's face at the moment the bullet made impact. But the layout of the magazine was telling. On the opposite page, facing Capa's picture, was a full-page advertisement for Vitalis, a men's hair cream, with a small picture of a man exerting himself at tennis and a larger picture of the

---

57. Sontag, *Regarding the Pain of Others*, 79.

58. For a discussion of Capa's photography, see R. Wheelan, *This Is War! Robert Capa at Work* (New York: International Center of Photography/Göttingen: Steidl, 2007).

FIGURE 3.2

Robert Capa. "The Falling Soldier." 1936. Photograph. (Credit: © International Center of Photography/Magnum Photos)

same man dressed in a white dinner jacket, his hair neatly parted and slicked down by the cosmetic product that was all the rage.[59] To be sure, not all images of suffering wind up next to advertisements for consumer products, but they do so with such regularity that we have to concede the truth of the tabloid guideline: "If it bleeds, it leads."[60]

Lest we be too dismissive of these images for their suggestion that suffering is simply an ordinary part of everyday life, no less and no more important than anything else that occupies our attention, I offer a second image for your consideration. [FIGURE 3.3] The Flemish painter Pieter Bruegel painted this large panorama of

---

59. Sontag, *Regarding the Pain of Others*, 32–33. For the Capa photograph juxtaposed with the Vitalis advertisement, see all-art.org/history658_photography13-18.html (accessed July 2020).

60. Sontag, *Regarding the Pain of Others*, 18. As one example, Sontag cites the advertising campaign mounted by Benetton, the Italian manufacturer of casual clothing, which used a photograph of the blood-stained shirt of a dead Croatian soldier to market a new fall line of clothes (120).

FIGURE 3.3

Pieter Bruegel the Elder. *The Carrying of the Cross* (*The Procession to Calvary*). 1564. Oil on oak. Kunsthistorisches Museum, Vienna, Austria. (Credit: Wikimedia Commons, PD-1925)

Christ carrying the cross in 1564.[61] The picture swarms with an assortment of very ordinary (pie-faced, snaggle-toothed, wart-nosed) people—more than 500 have been counted—who are engaged in the incidental affairs of everyday life. Along the top at the right, a man stoops down to pick up his cap; at the left, two small children stand as if lost in thought amid the commotion all around them; in the lower right-hand corner, a girl approaches a puddle, hikes up her skirt, and gestures for help as she wades through to a boy who has already crossed. [FIGURE 3.4] The scenery—the prominent rocky crag with a windmill at the top and the rooftops of a medieval town, including the distant dome of a church—suggests an ordinary day in an ordinary Flemish town. At first sight, there is nothing to

---

61. For description and discussion of the work, I draw from J. Dillenberger, *Style and Content in Christian Art* (Nashville: Abingdon, 1965), 155–59; see further L. Silver, *Pieter Bruegel* (New York: Abbeville Press, 2011).

FIGURE 3.4

Pieter Bruegel the Elder. Detail of *The Carrying of the Cross* (man
picking up cap)

indicate that an extraordinary event is going on in the middle of all
this "normal" chaos.

On closer inspection, we see that the crowd is moving from left
to right, and as our eyes follow their route, we gradually recognize
two other objects: a tall torture wheel in the right foreground and
then, behind it and farther away, a gathering crowd, an open circle,
and three empty crosses in the middle. [FIGURE 3.5] Now we recognize the place. It is Golgotha. It is the Gospels' account of Jesus'
crucifixion, now being played out as no more than a popular form of
public entertainment.

Once we get our bearings, we begin to see more details, lost
before in the swirl of activity. In the right foreground, on a rocky
ledge, is a group that is set apart from the crowd. At the center of this
group sits Mary, the mother of Jesus—pale, elderly, and submissive
in her nun-like attire. John, the beloved disciple, tries to console and
comfort her. [FIGURE 3.6] Here, at the edge of crowd, grief is real

FIGURE 3.5

Pieter Bruegel the Elder. Detail of *The Carrying of the Cross* (torture wheel, three crosses).

and mourning is in process, but no one seems to notice. In the left middle ground, a group of soldiers threatens a man while his wife tries to hold him back from engaging them. It is Simon of Cyrene, whom the soldiers are compelling to carry Jesus' cross. [FIGURE 3.7] We look more closely, and we see the wife is wearing a rosary with a cross, which suggests she is a believer, but her actions betray her true fidelity—she tries to restrain her husband from getting involved in this scene, even if it would be an act of mercy for him to do so. Finally, we look toward the middle of the crowd, there at last to see the one figure that is at the center of the drama. Jesus has fallen beneath the weight of the cross, which is just behind a wagon. [FIGURE 3.8] The people around him are arguing among themselves, perhaps trying to figure out how to resolve this situation so the procession can continue. The wagon contains two other criminals who, like Jesus, are headed toward that distant hill with the waiting crosses. Now we realize that the impending death of these three is the reason the

FIGURE 3.6

Pieter Bruegel the Elder. Detail of *The Carrying of the Cross* (Mary and John)

FIGURE 3.7

Pieter Bruegel the Elder. Detail of *The Carrying of the Cross* (Simon of Cyrene)

FIGURE 3.8

Pieter Bruegel the Elder. Detail of *The Carrying of the Cross* (Jesus and the cross)

crowd has gathered, the reason they move almost irresistibly toward the hill of execution, but the journey they make together, Bruegel suggests, is really no different than any other.

It is the sixteenth-century version of *Life* magazine; pain and suffering and advertisements for Vitalis are all part of the same mix. *C'est la vie*, as the French say: "Such is life."

(3) Perhaps the soldier in Goya's picture looks on this corpse with pity. Perhaps he feels a measure of genuine regret that a life has been taken, that a wife somewhere has been widowed, that a child somewhere will grow up fatherless. Perhaps, in other words, the soldier looks and feels sympathy, even compassion for this "other" person who was once alive but is now dead. It is surely a good thing when one's nervous system produces feelings of compassion at the sight of grief and loss. Surely to be able to feel compassion for the misfortune of others enlarges our awareness of how much suffering there is in the world we share with others. Sontag makes the point as follows: "Someone who is perennially surprised that depravity

exists, who continues to feel disillusioned (even incredulous) when confronted with evidence of what humans are capable of inflicting in the way of gruesome, hands-on cruelties upon other humans, has not reached moral or psychological adulthood." "*No one*," she says, "*after a certain age has the right to this kind of innocence*, of superficiality, to this degree of ignorance, or amnesia."[62]

Compassion is, however, a rather fickle emotion. If, for example, this soldier has seen too much war already, too many deaths, his compassion may be dulled by over exposure. Since he is simply one soldier in a regiment of many, perhaps he feels there is nothing "we" can do—but who is the "we"?—and nothing "they" can do either—but who are the "they"? If he feels there is nothing anyone can do about wars that leave people dead, then his compassion, however real, will likely be transient. Sooner or later his compassion will slip toward boredom, apathy, cynicism.[63]

Perhaps this explains why Goya was so alarmed by the thought that in his day the atrocities of war had become little more than a spectacle. Looking at the pain of others had become routine: people have the satisfaction of looking without flinching, or they have the pleasure (if their compassion is stirred) of flinching.[64] Either way, they regard the other as someone whose pain and suffering is to be seen, not felt, not experienced. Goya intended his pictures of the "disasters of war" to awaken, to shock, indeed, to "wound the viewer."[65] Toward this end, he removes every hint of the spectacular from his images, any suggestion that might encourage viewers to fixate on the "art of suffering." He uses no colors except black and white; no landscape except an atmosphere, a darkness barely sketched in. He allows himself only one overt "artistic" device: a caption attached to each of the eighty-two images. It was a voice, more like a scream, that he hoped would reach out and grab the viewer. One caption declares, "One can't look" (*No se puede mirar*); another, "This is bad" (*Esto es malo*); another, "This is worse" (*Esto es peor*); another, "This is the worst!" (*Esto es lo peor*); another, "What madness!" (*Que locura!*);

---

62. Sontag, *Regarding the Pain of Others*, 114 (emphasis added).

63. Ibid., 101.

64. Ibid., 41.

65. Ibid., 44.

another, "This is too much!" (*Fuerte cosa es!*); and another, "Why?" (*Por qué?*). [FIGURES 3.9, 3.10, 3.11] If the Gospel writer of Luke were writing the captions, one might read these words under one of the images: "Look at my hands and feet . . . . Touch me and see!" (Luke 24:39).

Compassion is indeed a fickle emotion. It not only slips toward impotent voyeurism ("It's terrible, but what can we do?"); it may also drift toward impertinent claims of innocence.[66] If, for example, the soldier is convinced that he is on the side of right, that his cause is just, then he may be persuaded that he is without blame.

FIGURE 3.9

Francisco de Goya. "One Can't Look." *The Disasters of War*. 1810–1820. Etching, burnished lavis, drypoint, and burin. National Gallery of Art, Washington, DC. (Credit: Wikimedia Commons, PD-US)

---

66. Ibid., 102. See further Mieke Bal's sharp critique of the way viewers often do no more than "traffic in pain" when looking at images of suffering: "It is the problem of sentimentality, of an identification that *either appropriates someone else's pain or exploits it* to feel oneself feeling at a time when the overflow of visual representations of suffering tends to inure one to the confrontation—and thus to feel good about oneself. The resulting exchange is too unfair—twenty years ago this man was dying, and I am enjoying myself at a photography exhibition. And I am the one to benefit? Something is just not right." ("Beautiful Pain," in *Beautiful Suffering: Photography and the Traffic in Pain*, 94; emphasis added)

FIGURE 3.10

Francisco de Goya. "This Is Worse." *The Disasters of War.* 1810–1820.
Etching. Museo Nacional del Prado, Madrid, Spain. (Credit: Wikimedia
Commons, PD–US)

FIGURE 3.11

Francisco de Goya. "Why?" *The Disasters of War.* 1810–1820. Etching,
lavis, drypoint, burin, and burnisher. National Gallery of Art, Washington, DC. (Credit: Wikimedia Commons, PD–US)

Patriotism trumps most all ambiguities, for in war the lines between good and evil are clearly drawn. There is a "we" and there is a "them." Either you are with us, or you are the enemy. There is no middle ground. Whatever sympathy there may be for the casualties of a just war, no moral guilt attaches to the execution of justice.

The French soldier is, after all, carrying out his duties in a foreign land. He looks on someone else's death, some "other" who has given his life for some Spanish cause, against which he, as a good citizen of France, has been conscripted to act. Like Pilate, the Roman governor assigned to the benighted and backward outpost of Judea, perhaps the soldier simply washes his hands of the whole sordid affair. It is someone else's problem, not his. Like the Auschwitz commandant who spends his days executing Jews for the Reich, this soldier will one day return home to evenings by the fire with his wife and children, perhaps listening to the orchestral works of Berlioz while he enjoys the safety and sanctity of his own self-constructed little world.

You may think I have now gone too far, that the connections I suggest between the French soldier looking on this dead Spanish body, Pilate looking on the disfigured body of the Jew named Jesus, the Auschwitz commandment watching the bodies of enemies of the Reich being shoved into the furnaces, . . . and us looking at other people's pain and suffering are too extreme. But here again, I take my cue from Sontag, who cites an example that seems to confirm we would all be more comfortable with simply washing our hands and pretending that the problem is somebody else's. She notes that modern society has elected to "honor" the suffering of European Jewry in the 1930s and 1940s, for example, by building "memory museums" that archive the horrors of our time: Yad Vashem in Jerusalem; the Jewish Museum in Berlin; the Holocaust Memorial Museum in Washington, D.C. In these places, which perhaps you have visited, we "house" the memorabilia of the Shoah. We walk past the display cases and the exhibits, chronologically organized. We look, we listen to the audiotape that narrates our tour, we remember, we regret, and we go back home, perhaps changed by what we have seen, perhaps not. But why, Sontag asks, is there not already in our nation's capital, which happens to be a city whose population is predominantly African American, a Museum of the History of

Slavery? Sontag's assessment of the way our selective memorializing of history absolves us from responsibility should cause us to flinch:

> To have a museum chronicling the great crime of African slavery in the United States of America would be to acknowledge that the evil was *here*. Americans prefer to picture the evil that was *there*, and from which the United States—a unique nation, one without any certifiably wicked leaders throughout its entire history—is exempt. That this country, like every other country, has its tragic past does not sit well with the founding and still all-powerful belief in American exceptionalism.[67]

I return to the point with which I began: compassion is a fickle emotion. It may slip toward feelings of boredom, cynicism, apathy—all different verses of the same song: impotence ("What can we do?"). Or it may slip toward self-righteousness, feigned as impertinent sympathy for someone else's problem. Either way, whatever compassion the French soldier may feel for the dead soldier who hangs before him, it will wither into something else, unless he translates what he feels into action; unless he gets up and closes the distance between him and the one he looks at; unless he learns that the "other" person who suffers is not only someone to be seen but also someone who (like himself) sees and feels.

III. LOOKING ON THROUGH THE EYES OF THE DEAD MAN

I invite you to imagine yourself into the soul of this dead man hanging from the tree. What does he see? What does he feel? What would he tell us, if he could only open his mouth and speak as he used to be able to do? (See Figure 3.1.) I know this may seem impossible for us to do, for after all dead people do not talk. In a real sense, they have "crossed over into a borderland of hurt where no one [can] follow."[68] As Emily Dickinson has put it, "Death . . . is exempt from change":

---

67. Sontag, *Regarding the Pain of Others*, 88. Since the publication of Sontag's book in 2003, the Smithsonian Institution's National Museum of African American History and Culture opened in Washington D.C. in 2016.

68. I take this suggestive quote from P. Conroy, *Beach Music* (New York: Doubleday, 1995), 559.

All but Death, can be Adjusted—
Dynasties repaired—
Systems—settled in their Sockets—
Citadels—dissolved—

Wastes of lives—resown with Colors
By Succeeding Springs—
Death—unto itself—Exception—
Is exempt from Change—[69]

Surely she is right. From a purely literal point of view, "death cannot be adjusted." Biologically speaking, death "*is* exempt from change."

To stretch our imaginations, I offer you this visual, a 1992 photograph by Jeff Wall, suggestively titled "Dead Troops Talk (A Vision After an Ambush of a Red Army Patrol Near Moqor, Afgahanistan, Winter 1986)."[70] [FIGURE 3.12] The picture is a Cibachrome transparency, seven and half feet high and more than thirteen feet wide, mounted on a light box. It is a staged photograph, constructed in the artist's Canadian studio. Wall was never in Afghanistan. He did not see what he photographs. The figures are realistic, but Wall has to imagine what these dead men might say to each other.

He depicts thirteen Russian soldiers in heavy winter uniforms and high boots. Their bodies are scattered across a war-blasted, blood-splashed slope littered with shell casings and crumpled metal. The men are dead but not yet buried. A few of them still have their helmets on. One kneeling figure talks animatedly, his head oozing red brain matter. Some slouch, leaning on an elbow, or sit, chatting, their opened skulls and handless arms in full view. One man bends over another who lies on his side as if asleep, perhaps encouraging him to sit up. Three men are playing around: one with a huge stomach wound sits astride another, lying prone, who is laughing

---

69. E. Dickinson, "# 749," in T. Johnson, ed., *The Complete Poems of Emily Dickinson* (New York: Little, Brown, and Company, 1961), 367.

70. For the description of the scene that follows below, I draw from Sontag, *Regarding the Pain of Others*, 123–26, and from the online room guide to *Jeff Wall Photographs 1978–2004* at Tate Modern, 21 October 2005–2008, tate.org.uk/ whats-on/tate-modern/exhibition/jeff-wall/jeff-wall-room-guide/jeff-wall-room-guide-room-8 (Figure 1).

FIGURE 3.12

Jeff Wall. "Dead Troops Talk" (a vision after an ambush of a Red Army
patrol, near Moqor, Afghanistan, winter 1986). 1992. Transparency in
lightbox, 229.0 x 417.0 cm. Courtesy of the artist.

at a third man who kneels before him dangling a strip of human
flesh. Another soldier, helmeted and legless, turns toward a distant
friend and smiles. Below him are two other soldiers, lying still; their
bloodied heads hanging over a rocky incline suggest they are not
quite ready for this make-believe resurrection.

In the midst of this surreal scene, the living go about their business very much as usual. At the far left, an Afghan soldier rifles
through a dead man's kit, perhaps hoping to find something he can
sell for profit. At the top right, two other Afghans head down the
path to join in the scavenging. At their side hang Kalashnikov rifles,
which they may have already stripped from other dead Russians, who
obviously no longer need them.

Wall suggests that the living may well be unconcerned about
what these dead men seem to be saying to each other. And perhaps
these dead men might be understood as equally disinterested in these
living ones who were part of the force that took their lives. They
are only looking at and talking to each other. They do not seem to
be denouncing the Russian war-makers who are picking over their
remains. Neither are they yelling at us in order to get our attention.
Frank Möller makes the point as follows:

These dead are supremely uninterested in the living: in those who
took their lives; in witnesses—and in us. And why should they
be interested in us? After all, what do they expect from us? Like
Rwanda, the Western public has never been particularly interested
in Afghanistan and its war . . . . If Wall's joking and smiling dead
move us, we move on.[71]

Even so, for the sake of discussion, imagine that they are looking at
us, that they are talking to us. What might they say? What would we
be able to hear?

If they were to tell us about the loss they feel on the other side of
death, could we, would we, understand? If we imagine them talking
about their children whose adult lives they will never see, would we
understand? If we were to eavesdrop on them talking about their
funeral, as if they had just finished watching it from the other side of
the grave, how would we describe for them what family and friends
felt as they grieved their passing? If they were to try to explain to us
what it felt like to lose life, to have the days on their calendar erased
by something they did not choose—a bullet, a sword, a disease, an
unforeseen tragedy—could we understand?

Sontag begins her ruminations by reminding us that "No 'we'
should be taken for granted when the subject is looking at other
people's pain."[72] After tracking this thought through the length of
her book, she ends by discussing Wall's photograph, with its evoca-
tion of the idea that these dead soldiers are talking to one another.
She notes, as I did a moment ago, that Wall does not depict these
soldiers as looking out of the picture at us, the viewers. They do not
seem at all interested in getting our attention. Then, like Möller who
was cited above, she raises this question: "Why should they seek our
gaze?"[73] What could we possibly understand about this scene? What
could we, who have never experienced anything like what they have
gone through, hear even if they were to call out to us? Her answer
is that we *cannot understand* how terrifying is the loss of someone
else's life. As onlookers, we *cannot imagine* what pain and suffering

---

71. Möller, "The Looking/Not Looking Dilemma," 794.

72. Sontag, *Regarding the Pain of Others*, 7.

73. Ibid., 125.

feels like to those who wear its wounds on their own bodies. I am persuaded that she is right, at least to a point. To *assume* that we know, really know, what the pain of another feels like is in the end to trivialize pain, to make it generic, as if one size, one dosage, fits all. As Shakespeare's young Benedict complains to his brother Don Pedro, who pretends to understand the depths of his suffering, "Everyone can master a grief but he that has it."[74]

And yet . . . and yet . . . even as I yield to the truth in Sontag's assessment, I am unsettled. I flinch at what it seems to mean. This world is full of people who are hurting. All around us there seem to be wounded ones calling out in the hope that someone will hear, even if from a distance; that someone will come to their aid, even if they do not fully understand what is being asked of them; that someone will offer comfort, even if they do not know why they should do so, let alone if anything they offer will do any good. This is the reality of the world we live in, and this reality does not change simply because we refuse to acknowledge it. Where pain and suffering are concerned, we do not have the luxury of patronizing reality. As we take comfort in our safe little provincial worlds, someone somewhere is wondering where we went.

My wincing at this thought becomes more acute, not less, when I take the first steps on the Lenten journey. Why must the route go through the memory of that last supper with Jesus, when he takes bread and *breaks it*, takes wine and *pours it* out, and then gives them to you and me with the warning that one of us will betray him? Why did he not offer us food that would invite us to remember the promise that life would ultimately triumph over death? Perhaps a puff pastry filled with honey? Why must the route lead into Gethsemane, through the memory of disciples who fall asleep and then run away at the moment of crisis? Why must it lead to Golgotha? Could we not just complete the journey by going directly to Jerusalem, where the choir is already singing "Hallelujah, Christ is risen. He is risen indeed"? Why do we have to stop off and see the crucifixion first? And why, after we have slogged through all of this, does Luke pile on by saying that even after we have remembered all these things, Jesus appears once more, just as we are beginning to get our bearings in

---

74. *Much Ado About Nothing*, III, ii, 28-29.

this world where disappointment and loss seem to be the new norm, and say, "Look at my hands and feet . . . . Touch me and see"? I do not know about you, but it is not hard for me to understand why Luke reports that the disciples "were startled and terrified"; that they were flooded by an uneven mixture of both joy and disbelief at the same time (Luke 24:37, 41).

IV. "WERE YOU THERE?"

In my confessional tradition, one of the songs we sing as we make this Lenten journey toward the empty tomb is the nineteenth-century Negro spiritual titled "Were You There?"

> Were you there when they crucified my Lord? . . .
> Were you there when they nailed him to the tree? . . .
> Were you there when they laid him in the tomb? . . .
> Were you there when he rose up from the grave? . . .

The first and most obvious answer to each of these questions is, "No," we were not there. Even if we should imagine ourselves as one of Jesus disciples, one of those who stood on the margins of the crowd that gathered outside Pilate's headquarters, we might have to concede that in truth we were not there; most of us were like Peter, watching from a safe distance, hoping not to be recognized as one of his followers. If a woman should happen to see us lurking in the shadows and say, "This one was also with him," we too would likely deny it. With Peter we hear ourselves saying, "Woman, I do not know him" (Luke 22:57; cf. John 18:17).

But the slow, rumbling chorus that keeps interrupting these questions seems to beg for a different response. "Oh! Sometimes it causes me to tremble, tremble, tremble." The words "tremble, tremble, tremble" call for a response that flows not out of the brain, where knowledge is cerebral and abstract, but out of the central nervous system, which turns knowledge into palpable action. The brain tells us the flame is hot; the nervous system triggers the hand and we move. Just so, the four verses of this song seem to be raising a question for the brain to contemplate: can you imagine what pain and suffering feels like? The chorus assumes that if we have walked the route Jesus mapped out for us, then we ought to be able not only to imagine this; we ought also to be able to feel the pain and wince, because it has left its mark on us.

Imagine for a moment that we are all doubting Thomases, and that like him, we who make this Lenten journey receive the resurrected Christ's invitation, "Put your finger here . . . reach out your hand and put it in my side" (John 20:27). [FIGURE 3.13] As in Caravaggio's *Doubting Thomas,* imagine Christ guiding your finger into his chest. Imagine what it would feel like to be inside, exploring Christ's wound, to retract the finger and see the blood on your hand. Look at Thomas's wrinkled brow. Watch as he clasps the hand of the other disciple who seems to be holding him round the waist, lest he fall headfirst into the wound that he probes so tentatively. What would your next move be? What would you say? The next time you see another innocent person's blood being spilled, will your nervous system respond with the memory of the spilt blood you have

FIGURE 3.13

Caravaggio (1571–1610). *Doubting Thomas.* 1602–1603. Oil on canvas. Sanssouci, Potsdam, Germany. (Credit: Wikimedia Commons, PD–US)

seen and touched? Will you only *think* about their suffering, or will you respond as one who has *seen* and *felt* their pain, because you are always on a journey toward the cross with a man named Jesus?

I leave you with two final images. The first is from the American poet Walt Whitman's (1819–1892) *Leaves of Grass*, a poem in celebration of the heroic human capacity to embody the noble virtues of compassion the world so desperately needs. Whitman began the poem in 1855, when he was thirty-six years old, but he continued to revise it with new additions until his death in 1892, at seventy-three years of age. During the Civil War he ministered to wounded soldiers in the Union Army in Washington, D.C. He remained there until 1873, when a stroke left him partially paralyzed. The words of his poem are not sacred, but they may be the gospel nonetheless:

> Agonies are one of my changes of garments,
> I do not ask the wounded person how he feels,
> I myself become the wounded person.
> My hurts turn livid upon me as I lean on a cane and observe.
>
> I am the mash'd fireman with breast-bone broken,
> Tumbling walls buried me in their debris,
> Heat and smoke I inspired, I heard the yelling shouts of my comrades,
> I heard the distant clicks of their picks and shovels,
> They have clear'd the beams away, they tenderly lift me forth.[75]

"Agonies are one of my changed garments. I do not ask the wounded person how he feels, I myself become the wounded person." Whitman's words evoke a second image, one we have already considered: Piero della Francesca's painting of *The Resurrection* (c. 1462–1464). (See Figures 2.5 and 2.6, full view and detail.) In the last presentation, we looked on della Francesca's depiction of Christ's face, eyes staring into the foreground with a firsthand memory of pain, as if to suggest that if Christ has experienced the resurrection, he has not yet comprehended its meaning. We looked on and listened to the commentary provided by Wallace Stegner, who used

---

75. W. Whitman, "Song of Myself," in *Walt Whitman: Leaves of Grass*, ed. J. Loving (Oxford, New York: Oxford University Press, 1990), 60.

this painting to frame an observation that now requires our attention once more. The truth and the promise of resurrection, Stegner writes, is that those who have died understand far more about life than those who have only lived.[76] The question before us now is, when we look on another's sufferings, should we ask them how they feel, or should we who have taken the broken bread and drunk the poured-out wine of the one we already know become the wounded person?

---

76. Stegner, *Crossing to Safety*, 221.

4

"Come Not When I Am Dead"

Our thoughts during this Lenten journey have been guided by two imperatives, both of which invite us to reflect on how we view the suffering of others. We began by looking at the first imperative. It is spoken by Pilate, who offers us the perspective of the outsider, the onlooker, the one who washes his hands of responsibility and then delivers a beaten Jesus over to the crowd to do with him as they wish. "Behold the man" (John 19:5), Pilate says, with the clear assumption that the next move is theirs and, by extension, ours. We heard the words. We looked at Pilate looking at Jesus. We looked at the crowd looking at Jesus. We looked at Jesus for ourselves, and we wondered, what are we supposed to see? What are we supposed to do? After all, we are only onlookers.

In the second presentation, we looked at the second imperative, which comes to us not from the onlooker but rather from the resurrected Christ, who knows firsthand what it means to experience suffering and loss. Luke's account of the journey to Emmaus suggests that Christ wants to share what he knows about suffering with his disciples. (See Figure 2.4, Caravaggio, *Supper at Emmaus*, 1605.) He says to them, "Look at my hands and feet . . . . Touch me and see" (Luke 24:39). We looked at the disciples looking at Jesus. We watched the joy, the terror, the doubt that played across their faces as they heard the words. We looked at Jesus looking at the disciples, each one pondering how to respond to the imperative. It seemed that Jesus was looking not only at them but also at us, for we would like to think that Jesus also counts us among those he calls his disciples. And so, as we wondered how they might respond, we could not help but wonder about ourselves. What are we supposed to see? If, like Thomas, we were to reach out and touch those hands and feet, what would we feel? (See Figure 3.13, Caravaggio, *Doubting Thomas*, 1602–1603.)

We reflected on both of these imperatives—"Behold the man" and "Touch me and see"—from the perspective of Susan Sontag's discernments in *Regarding the Pain of Others*. The picture she uses on the dustjacket of the book was our point of entry into her thinking. (See Figure 3.1, Francisco de Goya, "Not This!" *The Disasters of War*, 1810–1820.) A dead man hangs limp from the branch of tree. A soldier sits in repose, looking on the scene. The space between the two men is small, but the gap that separates the living from the dead seems immeasurable, and we are left to wonder what might be required to close the distance. What would it be like to see death through the knowing eyes of this Spanish soldier who has already died? What would it be like to see death through the eyes of this French soldier who can only look on from a distance? Do the two men see the same thing? Do they feel the same thing? Sontag cautions us not to assume anything: "No 'we' should be taken for granted when the subject is looking at other people's pain."[77] Sontag concludes that the distance between the living and the dead, between those who know firsthand what suffering feels like and those who look on it from a safe distance, is too great. In the end, we *cannot* understand, *cannot* imagine how terrifying, how painful it is to have suffered such loss and brokenness as the soldier who hangs lifeless from this tree.

And yet the Gospel of Luke insists that at the end of the Lenten journey, we will find ourselves standing before the resurrected Christ, who will say to all his disciples, "Look at my hands and feet, forever scarred by the nails of pain; Touch me and see for yourself what it feels like to be me" (cf. Luke 24:39). In this presentation, we resume our Lenten journey by returning to Piero della Francesca's depiction of the Resurrection. (See Figure 2.5, Piero della Francesca, *The Resurrection*,

---

77. Sontag, *Regarding the Pain of Others*, 7.

c. 1462–1464.) We look again at della Francesca's Christ, with one foot still in the tomb as if he has not yet fully stepped into life, and we wonder, what does it feel like to have died and then to have the chance to live again? We think on this question, and we remember the commentary from the novelist Wallace Stegner: "Those who have been dead understand things that will never be understood by those who have only lived."[78] I invite you now to focus on Jesus' right foot. In the final presentation, we will focus on the left foot, the foot that steps into life in the world on the other side of death, but first we must think about the foot that is still connected to death. We must ponder what Jesus wants to teach us about what it feels like to be dead.

For the duration of this presentation, I ask you to imagine what Jesus expects of us if we are to accompany him to Gethsemane, where he says to us, "I am deeply *grieved, even to death*, remain here, and *stay awake with me*" (Matt 26:38), then journey on with him to the cross, where the words "*grieved unto death*" and "*stay awake with me*" may require more of us than we imagine.

I. "HE DESCENDED INTO HELL"

To set the table, let me take us back to a scene just before the one della Francesca depicts. The Gospels report that Jesus made his way from the garden of Gethsemane to the cross. Countless artists have tried to depict the agony of the crucifixion. None has done so with more palpable expression than Matthias Grünewald, whose 1515 Isenheim altarpiece has been described by Sir Kenneth Clark as "the most corporeal of all Crucifixions."[79] [FIGURE 4.1] It is a polyptych, a multiple-sided altarpiece, that presents different scenes from the life of Christ. The two outer panels we see here show the crucifixion, with the entombment (not shown here) just below. When these two outer panels are opened, the annunciation and the

---

78. Stegner, *Crossing to Safety*, 221.

79. Cited in Dillenberger, *Style and Content in Christian Art*, 149. I draw on Dillenberger in the discussion that follows. See further D. L. Jeffrey, *In the Beauty of Holiness: Art and the Bible in Western Culture* (Grand Rapids: Eerdmans, 2017), 125–58 and Figures 44, 45; E. Falque, *The Guide to Gethsemane: Anxiety, Suffering, Death* (trans. G. Hughes; New York: Fordham University Press, 2018).

FIGURE 4.1

Matthias Grünewald (c. 1470–1528). *Crucifixion.* Isenheim Altarpiece. 1515. Oil on panel. Unterlinden Museum, Alsace, France. (Credit: Wikimedia Commons, PD–US)

resurrection can be seen on their back sides. Our reflections center on these now separated external panels of the crucifixion.

To the right of the cross stands John the Baptist, with the Scriptures in his left hand. With his right hand he points an exaggerated forefinger at Jesus. The Latin words, "He must increase, I must decrease," are inscribed against a black sky. At John's feet is a lamb, symbolic of sacrifice; one leg supports a slender reed cross; from the lamb's cut-open breast, blood flows into a chalice on the ground. To the left of the cross, John the beloved disciple supports in his arms Mary the mother of Jesus, who has been committed to his care. Her hands are clasped together, as if in prayer, as she looks on the scene and then collapses with grief that is more internal and imagined than displayed. The smaller figure kneeling at the foot of the cross is Mary

Magdalene. Her body leans backward in an "anguished arc."[80] Her head is tilted in a painful pose that exposes quivering cheeks and cascading hair that seems to enwrap her with grief. Like Mary the mother of Jesus, she raises clasped hands, but her fingers, a mirror image of Christ's fingers, are interlocked and extended upward in a gesture that suggests she is reaching out in an effort to close the distance between her and this One who had once healed her of evil spirits (Luke 8:2; cf. Mark 16:9).

It is of course the figure of Christ on the cross that commands our attention. Grünewald focuses on the scene in the Gospels when "Jesus bowed his head and gave up his spirit" (John 19:30; cf. Matt 27:50; Mark 15:37; Luke 23:46). If we follow the composite record from the Gospels, we remember Jesus' last words. Matthew reports that at three o'clock in the afternoon, as darkness fell over the whole land, Jesus cried out with a loud voice, "My God, my God, why have you forsaken me?" (Matt 27:46; cf. Mark 15:34; Ps 22:1). There was no answer. Then, according to John's Gospel, Jesus said, "I am thirsty" (John 19:28). The words recall Jesus' question to Peter in the garden of Gethsemane: "Am I not to drink the cup that the Father has given me?" (John 18:11). Jesus seems to be thirsting for God's cup, but what the onlookers offer is a sponge full of sour wine (vinegar). Having cried out "Why?" and gotten no answer, having thirsted for the cup that God offers and received only something sour, Jesus said, "It is finished" (John 19:30) and exhaled for the last time.

Grünewald captures the moment by asking us to look on Jesus' body stretched out on a roughhewn cross. His head rests lifelessly in the hollow caused by shoulder muscles torn from their joints. The torque of his body bends the crossbeam downward. His stomach, striped with nearly exposed rib bones, is sucked back toward the spinal cord; his right side leaks the blood drawn by the soldier's spear. His knees buckle; the anklebones are disjointed. But it is his hands that most capture our attention. The fingers are not placidly laid out in the familiar pose that suggests a serene blessing of the moment. Instead, they stretch out grotesquely, as if with the words "My God, my God, why?" Jesus is clawing at the heavens for an answer that does not come. [FIGURE 4.2]

---

80. Dillenberger, *Style and Content in Christian Art*, 145.

Matthew's Gospel reports that at the moment Jesus breathed his last breath, the curtain of the temple was torn in two, from top to bottom. The earth shook, and the rocks were split. The tombs also were opened, and many bodies of the saints who had fallen asleep were raised (Matt 27:51-52). Matthew's report of the opening of the graves is one of but a few oblique New Testament references to Jesus' descent into hell (cf. 1 Pet 3:19; 4:6). Despite the meager evidence of such a descent, many Christians affirm the claim as a statement of faith, especially in the Apostles' Creed (second century CE), which is part of the baptismal liturgy in Roman Catholic, Anglican, and Lutheran churches:

> I believe in God, the Father Almighty,
> maker of Heaven and earth;
> And in Jesus Christ his only Son our Lord;
> who was conceived by the Holy Ghost,
> born of the Virgin Mary,
> suffered under Pontius Pilate,
> was crucified, dead, and buried.
> *He descended into hell.*
> The third day he rose again from the dead.
> *He ascended into heaven,*
> and is seated at the right hand of God the Father Almighty.
> From thence he shall come to judge the quick and the dead.
> I believe in the Holy Ghost,
> the holy catholic Church,

FIGURE 4.2

Matthias Grünewald. Detail of *Crucifixion.*

the communion of saints,
the forgiveness of sins, the resurrection of the body,
and the life everlasting. (emphasis added)

The question the Apostles' Creed invites is, when Jesus descended into hell, what did he do there? The question evoked considerable speculation from early Christian writers (e.g., Ignatius, c. 50–107 CE; Bishop Melito of Sardis, died c. 190 CE), the Church Fathers (e.g., Aquinas, 1225–1274), and perhaps most famously, Dante (1265–1321; *Inferno*).[81]

The fullest and most interesting description of Jesus' descent into hell comes from the *Gospel of Nicodemus* (or *Acts of Pilate*), an apocryphal account (perhaps fourth century) that details Jesus' activities from the time of his passion to his ascension. This account of Jesus' descent begins with Joseph of Arimathea speaking in Jerusalem about how marvelous it was not only that Jesus himself was raised from the dead but also that he raised the righteous dead (the saints who died before Jesus) with him.[82] With considerable detail, the account describes the King of Glory entering Hades, seizing Satan, and handing him over to the angels to be bound with iron fetters (5 [21].3; 6 [22].2). Then the King of Glory stretches out his right hand to Adam and other righteous souls (including Moses and the prophets):

---

81. For discussion and images, see H. Hornik and M. Parsons, "The Harrowing of Hell," *BR* 19 (June 2003): 18–26, 50.

82. In Jesus' day, Hell (Sheol in Hebrew, Hades in Greek) was understood not as a place of eternal damnation but as a resting place for all dead souls. Christians believed that the righteous dead remained in this underworld until Jesus came; there was no heaven for them to go to until Jesus died and ascended; e.g., Ignatius (first century CE): "If then those who had walked in ancient practices attained unto newness of hope, no longer observing sabbaths but fashioning their lives after the Lord's day, on which our life also arose through Him and through His death which some men deny—a mystery whereby we attained unto belief, and for this cause we endure patiently, that we may be found disciples of Jesus Christ our only teacher—if this be so, how shall we be able to live apart from Him? seeing that even the prophets, being His disciples, were expecting Him as their teacher through the Spirit. And for this cause He whom they rightly awaited, when He came, raised them from the dead" (*To the Magnesians*, 9.1-2).

. . . the King of Glory stretched out his right hand, and took hold of our forefather Adam and raised him up. Then he turned also to the rest and said: "Come with me, all you who have suffered death through the tree which this man touched. For behold, I raise you all up again through the tree of the cross." With that he put them all out. And our forefather Adam was seen to be full of joy and said: "I give thanks to thy majesty, O Lord, because thou hast brought me up from the lowest (depth of) Hades." Likewise also all the prophets and the saints said: "We give thanks, O Christ, Saviour of the world, because thou hast brought up our life from destruction."

When they had said this, the Saviour blessed Adam with the sign of the cross on his forehead. And he did this also to the patriarchs and prophets and martyrs and forefathers, and he took them and leaped out of Hades. And as he went the holy fathers sang praises, following him and saying, "Blessed be he who comes in the name of the Lord. Alleluia [Ps 118:26]. To him be the glory of all the saints." (*Gospel of Nicodemus, Acts of Pilate*, 8[24].1-2)[83]

This list of resurrected saints proved very influential for Byzantine, Medieval, and Renaissance artists, who painted these and a host of other biblical figures communing with Jesus in hell, then ascending with him to life beyond the grave.

One example is the large altarpiece of *Christ in Limbo* (1552) for the Church of Santa Croce in Florence by the Italian artist Agnolo Bronzino.[84] [FIGURE 4.3] In the thinking of the day (largely influenced by the theology of Aquinas), hell was divided into levels. In this painting, those on the bottom level have not yet been redeemed, and so they look at or reach longingly for the Savior, who holds a banner of victory in his hand as he stands on the door of hell, in the hope that they will be included in the resurrection. Those on the upper level, with or above Jesus, have already been or are being raised. To Jesus' left are Adam and Eve. John the Baptist stands just above

---

83. "The Gospel of Nicodemus. Acts of Pilate and Christ's Descent into Hell," in *New Testament Apocrypha*. Vol. 1, 524.

84. See further T. Zeigler, "Altered Context: Bronzino's *Descent of Christ into Limbo*," in A. M. Galdy, ed., *Agnolo Bronzino: Medici Court Artist in Context* (Cambridge: Cambridge Scholars Publishers, 2014), 81–106.

FIGURE 4.3

Agnolo Bronzino (1503–1572). *Descent of Christ into Limbo.* 1552. Fresco. Refectory of Basilica of Santa Croce, Italy. (Credit: Wikimedia Commons, CCA-SA 2.0)

them and to the right. To the right of John the Baptist stands the good thief, Dysmas, still bearing the cross on which he was executed alongside Jesus. To Jesus' right, Moses, with a short pair of horns on his head, holds the Ten Commandments; behind him is David with his harp; and behind David is the prophet Isaiah, holding a saw, which according to apocryphal accounts was the instrument of his martyrdom.

A still more suggestive painting is Vittore Carpaccio's *Meditation on the Passion of Christ* (c. 1490). [FIGURE 4.4] Carpaccio (1450–1525) was born in Venice, where he studied for a time with Giovanni Bellini.[85] His *Meditation on the Passion of Christ* is now located in the Metropolitan Museum of Art in New York. In the foreground of this painting, Carpaccio places three figures. Seated on the left is Jerome. Opposite him on the right is Job. Like his counterpart, Job is seated. His posture indicates his meditation on the central figure of Christ, who slumps in Job's direction as he awaits the coming resurrection. The background provides two contrasting views of the landscape. To the left, just above Christ's throne, is a dead tree, crooked toward a deserted mountain trail where a leopard is about to devour a doe. The imagery suggests a world of death, unrestrained force, and hapless victims. To the right, the imagery suggests just the opposite: the trees and plants are full with foliage; walled villages are safe and secure; a leopard walks peacefully behind a doe; a red bird sits unafraid on the ground.

It is the figure of Job that deserves attention. Carpaccio suggests that he is among the saints who commune with Jesus during his time between life and death. He places Job on the side where life and peace and promise define the landscape. Yet there are also signs that death remains a real presence for Job. A shattered human skull along with dried-out bone pieces lie on the ground beneath his feet. A piece of the granite-like block, broken off at the bottom, supports him. Job supports his weary head in the palm of his left hand while pointing with his right finger to the sandals on his feet. Carpaccio seems to be

---

85. On Bellini and Carpaccio, see H. Hornik, "The Venetian Images by Bellini and Carpaccio: Job as Intercessor or Prophet?" *Review and Expositor* 99 (2002): 541–68.

FIGURE 4.4

Vittore Carpaccio (1450–1525). *Meditation on the Passion of Christ.* c. 1490. Oil and tempera on wood. Metropolitan Museum of Art, New York, NY. (Credit: John Stewart Kennedy Fund, 1911)

calling attention to Job's feet, which have had to walk through the hurtful debris of a life that once seemed to hold so much promise.

The imagery of Job pointing to his feet provides a suggestive parallel to Luke's account of Jesus' post-resurrection appearance to the disciples on the road to Emmaus (Luke 24). *After* the disciples had recognized him, *after* they had broken bread with him, *after* they had proclaimed the post-Easter hallelujah—"The Lord has risen indeed!" (24:35)—Jesus came and stood in their midst to speak one further word of instruction: "Look at my hands and my feet . . . . Touch me and see" (24:39). It seems a rather odd thing to say to those who have already experienced his resurrection and have already begun to proclaim its promise for others, *unless* perhaps Jesus is concerned to remind them one last time that even in the afterglow of resurrection it is imperative that those who proclaim the gospel be able to touch and feel the raw hurt of brokenness and loss. Job points to his feet, much like Jesus may have done with the disciples. The evocative difference here is that it is *Job who directs Jesus* to take one last look before resurrection becomes a reality. Carpaccio suggests that when Jesus descended into hell, during the crucial interval when Jesus was preparing to ascend, Job was one of the saints who was teaching Jesus something important about what it means to walk where the Jobs of the world have walked.[86]

II. WHAT DOES JOB HAVE TO TEACH JESUS ABOUT LIFE ON THE OTHER SIDE OF DEATH?

Job's story is complex and fraught with many difficulties. No *Reader's Digest* summary can possibly do it justice. That said, the basic plotline of the story unfolds as follows.[87]

The book begins by describing Job as an unparalleled exemplar of virtue and faith. By God's own assessment, "there is no one like him in all the earth" (Job 1:8). This assessment rests on the three-fold affirmation of Job (once by the narrator [1:8] and twice by God [1:8; 2:3]) as a "blameless and upright man who fears God and turns away from evil." His righteousness is confirmed by his full family and his contingent of servants and possessions (1:2-3). In sum, the beginning of the book depicts Job as a kind of pre-fall Adam person, someone who lives in a seemingly perfect, Eden-like world, free of corruption from any source.

Then the bottom falls out of Job's world. He loses his possessions, his servants, and, most grievously, his family—seven sons and three daughters are dead, as the text puts it, "for no reason" (Job 2:3). As he sits on an ash heap of suffering, three friends—Eliphaz, Bildad, and Zophar—come to "console" and "comfort" him, only to discover that they have no words, at least at the outset, that are equal to the challenge his suffering presents. They sit with him in silence for seven days and seven nights, for, as the text says, "they saw

---

86. For further discussion, see S. E. Balentine, "Who Will Be Job's Redeemer?" *Perspectives in Religious Studies* 26 (1999): 269–89.

87. In what follows, I draw from my commentary, *Job* (Smyth & Helwys Bible Commentary; Macon, GA: Smyth and Helwys, 2006).

that his suffering was very great" (Job 2:11-13). What, after all, can people say to someone when life pushes them beyond Eden into a borderland of hurt?

Job is the first to break this silence, and his words send shock waves through the friends' world of settled convictions. Job had previously known little if anything firsthand about suffering and loss; now he has become intimate with its claims. When he speaks about suffering from the ash heap, he speaks not as an outsider but as an insider. Out of the depths of pain and brokenness, Job opens his mouth and he *curses* the life he was born into—Damn the day on which I was born; damn the night on which I was conceived (3:1-10)—and he *protests*, with a repetition of the thunderous question "Why?" (3:11, 12, 20; cf. vv. 16, 23). In view of what he has lost—seven sons, three daughters, dead "for no reason" (2:3)—it would be less than honest to speak in any other way. Perhaps his curses will not change anything; perhaps his questions are absurd; perhaps they can never be answered. Even so, the words of grief and rage signal his resolve not to be a passive onlooker in the face of death and destruction. Perhaps his words are a radical act of faith, because Job refuses to believe that this is the way life is supposed to be.

Job's friends must now decide how to respond. As long as Job had been content to suffer in silence, they were content to sit with him, to "console" and "comfort" him with their sympathetic presence (Job 2:11-13). Once he begins to curse and complain, everything changes. We may visualize their transition by placing two of William Blake's etchings side by side. [FIGURES 4.5, 4.6]

In the first etching, Job sits on a mound of straw, his head resting on his wife's breast. His hands, palms downward, extend by his side. His wife kneels behind him, her body providing a pillar of support, her uplifted hands gesturing the prayer Job himself seems too exhausted to offer. The six uplifted hands of the friends mimic the wife, although their reach heavenward is more extended and their facial expressions convey more intensity and emotion. It is as if by the force of their gestures they wish to lift Job safely out of his distress and into the arms of God. At the top and bottom of the frame Blake has inscribed words from Job 2:12: "When they lifted up their eyes afar off and knew him not they lifted up their voices and wept . . . ." To these words Blake adds a quotation from James

FIGURE 4.5

William Blake (1757–1827). *Book of Job*. Plate 7: "Job's Comforters," from *Illustrations of the Book of Job*. 1825–1826. Engraving. Metropolitan Museum of Art, New York, NY. (Credit: Gift of Edward Berment, 1917)

FIGURE 4.6

William Blake (1757–1827). *Book of Job*. Plate 10: "Job Rebuked by His Friends," from *Illustrations of the Book of Job*. 1825–1826. Engraving. Metropolitan Museum of Art, New York, NY. (Credit: Gift of Edward Berment, 1917)

5:11, which provides the catchword—"patience"—that captures not only the popular understanding of Job's exemplary faith but also the reason for the friends' sympathetic support: "Ye have heard of the patience of Job and have seen the end of the Lord, that the Lord is very pitiful, and of tender mercy" (AV).

In the second etching, Blake's Job has moved from the ash heap to a kneeling position. No longer leaning backward, Job now holds himself upright, his stomach muscles taut, as if flexed in anticipation of a negative response to the curses he has just hurled into the silence of his world. His spotted torso is wrapped from the waist down with the traditional sackcloth. His head is tilted backward. His tear-stained eyes are fixed on the God above whom he cannot see but will not cease to trust. Job's solemn misery is suggested by the three citations of Scripture at the top of the frame:

> But he knoweth the way I take
> when he hath tried me I shall come forth like gold (Job 23:10)

> Have pity upon me! Have pity upon me! O ye my friends
> for the hand of God hath touched me (Job 19:21)

> Though he slay me yet will I trust in him (Job 13:15)

But the friends have ceased to play the role of comforter. They are now Job's inquisitors. With outstretched hands they point fingers of ridicule in Job's direction. The expressions on their faces are now cold and hard, as is particularly clear in the face of the friend to the fore, presumably Eliphaz. Job's wife, whose right hand is also partially extended, seems now to have joined in the reproach. Two further citations in the bottom of the frame from Job's last speech in the first cycle indicate what has drawn the friends' ire:

> The Just Upright man is laughed to scorn (Job 12:4)

> Man that is born of a Woman is of few days & full of trouble
> he cometh up like a flower & is cut down, he fleeth also as a shadow
> & continueth not. And dost thou open thine eyes upon such a one
> & bringest me into judgment with thee (Job 14:1-3)

The friends make their case against Job in three cycles of speeches (Job 4–14; 15–21; 22–27). The general theme in the first cycle (chs. 4–14) is God's moral governance of the world, especially as this is manifest in God's unfailing care for the righteous and God's equally unfailing punishment of the wicked (4:7-11; 8:8-19; 11:11). The friends' initial approach to Job suggests that they have read the required text for Pastoral Care 101. Like kind and sympathetic counselors, they each gently raise a series of rhetorical questions, questions they trust will nudge Job to answers they already know. Eliphaz, always the lead spokesman, sets the tone the others will follow with his first questions:

> If one ventures a word with you, will you be offended?
>> Forgive me, but who can keep from speaking? (4:2)

> Is not your fear of God your confidence,
>> and the integrity of your ways your hope?
> Think now, who that was innocent ever perished?
>> Or where were the upright cut off? (4:6-7)

With equal measures of comfort and encouragement, the friends are confident that Job will see things the way they do. If he will heed their counsel, they have no doubt that he too will discover that God can always be trusted to reward the righteous and punish the wicked. But when Job looks at the same world and claims that even the birds and the plants know things are more complicated than this (12:7-10), Eliphaz and his friends know they are in for a long day.

In the second round (chs. 15–21), the friends reduce their argument to the one truth they are certain Job will not dispute: the wicked (read Job) are always punished (15:17-35; 18:5-21; 20:4-9). From this point on they will dispense with any pretense of claiming that God always prospers the righteous. Their tone is now noticeably much sharper, a signal that they have stiffened their resolve to wrench a confession of guilt from Job. They offer no word of encouragement, hope, or promise to Job. Instead, they increase their warnings, double their rebukes, and up the ante he must pay if he continues to challenge the Judge of all the world. Once again, Eliphaz leads the way:

> You [Job] are doing away with the fear of God
> > and hindering meditation before God.
> For your iniquity teaches your mouth,
> > and you choose the tongue of the crafty,
> Your own mouth condemns you, not I,
> > your own lips testify against you. (15:4-6)

When Job counters with a question, one of many, that directly disputes their assertions—"How often then is the lamp of the wicked put out? How often then does calamity come upon them?" (21:17)—the friends know it is time to take off the gloves.

In the third round of speeches (chs. 22–27), the friends give up their efforts to coerce a confession from Job. Now, like Pilate, they wash their hands of the whole affair and simply pronounce Job guilty. Their notion of an orderly trial, with evidence so strong the defendant can only yield and agree to guilt, has not worked. But inasmuch as the friends claim the right to be both judge and jury in the case of God v. Job, they can still secure the desired outcome by simply ruling from the bench that Job is guilty beyond any reasonable doubt. Eliphaz takes the point for the last time: "Is not your wickedness great? There is no end to your iniquities" (22:5). Job has but one option, Eliphaz insists: "Agree with God, and be at peace" (22:21). Eliphaz's counsel bears a close resemblance to the advice Sam offers Berish in E. Wiesel's *The Trial of God.* Berish insists on bringing God to trial for the massacre of Jews in Shamgorod in 1649. Sam, who plays the role of God's defense attorney, warns Berish that God's justice is not subject to human critique.

> Why murder—why death? Pertinent questions. But we have some more: Why evil—why ugliness? If God chooses not to answer, He must have his reasons. God is God, and His will is independent of ours—as is His reasoning.

Berish has one choice, Sam says, and one choice only: "Endure. Accept. And say Amen."[88]

---

88. E. Wiesel, *The Trial of God* (New York: Schocken Books, 1979), 132.

In effect, the friends demand that Job surrender unconditionally to their theology: to wit, he is suffering, therefore he has sinned; he is guilty, therefore he must repent. This theology inscribes a rejection that recalls a painful scene from Wallace Stegner's short story, "Impasse." Having witnessed the rebuff of his beloved but homely daughter Margaret by yet another potential suitor, her father Louis muses to himself about the advice he might offer her.

> . . . what had happened so dramatically was forever beyond talk. He could never say to [Margaret], "I saw you invite him, and I saw him take one good look and pass." Could you say to your daughter, "Accept your looks for what they are?" Could you tell her, "You were born struck out, and it won't help to stand in the batter's box demanding that the pitcher throw you a fourth strike?"

Margaret's father cannot bring himself to tell his daughter that God determined willy-nilly, before she saw the first light of day, that she was "born struck out." "My God," he says, "she has *hope*. . . . Everybody young has hope."[89]

Eliphaz and his friends look on Job with no such panged restraints. Once the strategy to love Job into conformity with their theology has failed, they are left with but two options. They can rethink their definition of friendship. Could it be that Job deserves their loyalty, no matter his guilt or innocence? Or they can decide that their theology is more important than his friendship. When friends run afoul of theological orthodoxy, one must either convert them or condemn them. Eliphaz and his friends choose the latter course. To be charitable, we might imagine that they simply get tired of "being with" Job. Perhaps, as Martin Marty observes, sharing the grief of another, taking into oneself the "agony of the nerves exposed, the plotlessness of pain that never stops," is too much to ask of anyone. Most of those who wear the label of "friend," Marty suggests, will be "tempted to turn their backs" and retreat at some point.[90] Whether charitably viewed or not, we are left with the report that Job's "friends" have

---

89. W. Stegner, "Impasse," in *Collected Stories of Wallace Stegner* (New York: Penguin Books, 1991), 291.

90. M. Marty, *A Cry of Absence* (San Francisco: Harper and Row, 1983), 128.

condemned him as guilty. Charged and convicted, Job now waits alone for whatever comes next.

Job expects more from his friends. He does not wish to be left to suffer alone. His theology of friendship instructs all of us—and as Carpaccio's painting suggests, perhaps Jesus too—as to what those who are insiders to pain and suffering expect from us outsiders who simply look on from a safe distance. The clearest and most succinct expression of the friendship Job needs and expects is found in Job 6:14: "The despairing (*lammās*) needs loyalty (*ḥesed*) from a friend, even if (perhaps "when") they forsake the fear of the Almighty." Job expects *ḥesed* from a friend. The conventional translation of this word is "kindness" or "steadfast love." A better rendering is "loyalty." *Ḥesed* describes both an attitude and an action that binds two parties together in an unbreakable partnership. Its fullest meaning is exemplified by God, for whom "loyalty and faithfulness" (*ḥesed weʾemet*) are constant attributes (e.g., Pss 25:10; 57:3; 89:14; 138:2). God's loyalty is enacted; it is a disposition that is demonstrated. God "does" (*ʿāsâ*) *ḥesed* (e.g., Gen 24:12, 14; Exod 20:6 [= Deut 5:10]; 2 Sam 2:6; 1 Kgs 3:6; Jer 9:24 [MT 9:23]), the most tangible evidence of which is God's commitment to "keeping covenant and steadfast love" (*šōmer habberît weḥaḥesed*; Deut 7:9, 12; 1 Kgs 8:23 [= 2 Chr 6:14]; Neh 1:5; 9:32; Dan 9:4). When humans fail God and break the covenant partnership, it is "loyalty and faithfulness" that motivates God to restore it (Exod 34:6).

What Job hopes for from his friends is a loyalty that will not let go of him, even if suffering pushes him beyond the boundaries of conventional piety ("the fear of the Almighty"). What he receives from them is quite different (6:15-21). His friends are "treacherous" (*bāgĕdû*). The imagery suggests "deceit." They are "brothers," which implies that they are connected to him by a familial affection and solidarity, but they have abandoned him. They are inconsistent and unreliable. Job compares them to the seasonal wadis of Palestine. In the rainy season when water is plentiful, they are full to overflowing. But when the heat of summer arrives, and water is needed and scarce, they dry up and disappear (6:15-17). Job compares his own disappointment at their failure to provide what he needs to that of parched caravaneers who spy out the promise of water in the desert but, upon arrival, find it to be only a mirage (6:18-20). Like these dried-up, empty waterbeds, the friends have become for Job a nonexistent resource. The Hebrew of verse 21 says, literally, "you have become nothing (*lōʾ*)." With a final play on words, Job adds, "you see (*tirʾû*) a calamity, and you are afraid (*tîrāʾû*)."

Job's friends look at him sitting on the ash heap and they "see" that "his suffering is very great" (2:13). But they do not see "*him.*" Instead, they see a "*calamity*," that is, they see a *problem* to be solved, an *issue* to be pondered, but they do not see the person. They do not feel his pain; they merely abstract theories about suffering from the case study he provides. They talk about issues. They theologize, but they do not "comfort" and "console." As the French philosopher and activist Simone Weil (1909–1943) observed, violence turns every-body subjected to it into a "thing."[91]

Job's friends encounter him like the friends Barbara Brown Taylor speaks about in an article published in *Christian Century.* Because she is an Episcopalian priest, a distinguished Professor of Religion and Philosophy (at Piedmont College), a bestselling author, and, according to Baylor University, "one of the ten most effective preachers in the English-speaking world," Barbara Brown Taylor is a presence hard to miss in the small community of Clarkesville, Georgia, where she lives. She writes of running into friends and acquaintances while grocery shopping and the like. In the aftermath of the election of Rev. Gene Robinson as the first openly gay bishop in the Anglican Communion, they stop her to ask what her *position* is as a Christian on the vexing problem of homosexuality. The ques-tion basically leaves her speechless. She says that she doesn't have a *position*, but she does know *people* who suffer the ridicule, abuse, and general ill will that others show toward them. To reduce these persons to a *position* or an *issue*, she says, seems irreverent, "like operating on someone's body without looking at him in the face."

She loves the Bible and happily affirms that she has spent more than half her life trying to practice its teachings. But a peculiar thing happens to her when she reads the Bible. As she practices what she

---

91. S. Weil, "The Iliad, or Poem of Might," reprinted from *Intimations of Christi-anity among the Ancient Greeks* (1957) in *The Simone Weil Reader*, ed. G. Panchias (New York: David McKay Co., 1977), 153–83.

learns in the Bible, she says the Bible keeps turning its back on her, as if trying to push her away, out into the world where the word must be made flesh, even if it means loving the "wrong people" after you have been warned time and again to stop. She concludes her article with these words about where reading the Bible leads her: "I do not know what is right. All I know is whom I love, and how far I must go before there is no one left whom I do not love. If I am wrong, then I figure the Word of God will know what to do with me. I am betting my life on that."[92]

III. "Look at Me and Be Appalled"

What is required of us if we are to be Job's friends? If we are to move beyond theories that try to explain suffering to comforting and consoling and loving those whom life has consigned to the ash heap? I am struck by the fact that Job repeatedly asks his friends to *look* at him and *listen carefully* to his words:

> Be pleased to look at me (Job 6:28)
> Listen carefully to my words (Job 13:17; 21:2)
> Look at me and be appalled, and lay your hand on your mouth (Job 21:5)

The friends have the advantage, if we may call it that, of looking on Job's suffering from a safe distance. This distance allows them to be glib about what it feels like to be Job. Eliphaz, for example, seems entirely too impassive when he urges Job to accept hurt and brokenness as if it can be dismissed with a simple creedal affirmation:

> How happy is the one whom God reproves;
>   therefore do not despise the discipline of the Almighty.
> For he wounds, but he binds up;
>   he strikes, but his hands heal. (Job 5:17-18)

For Eliphaz, the pain of being wounded and struck is unfelt and virtually invisible. When he and the friends look at Job, they see only the distant promise of healing. They feel nothing so deeply as their

---

92. B. Brown Taylor, "Where the Bible Leads Me," *The Christian Century*, February 9, 2004.

conviction that in due course the pain will go away. In the meantime, Job should be pleased that God loves him enough to hurt him.

Job insists that the intensity of his suffering, the very physicality of his pain, requires the friends to look again. His suffering is real; his grief over dead children who no longer laugh at his dinner table is not abstract or imaginary. It is visceral; it takes palpable shape in wounds that scream and cannot be silenced. The pain is constant, not temporary; what has been lost cannot be restored—his children are dead; they cannot be replaced with substitutes. His pain is massive, not minor or trifling; it cannot be fixed with a bandage. Job would remind Eliphaz and all contemporary sympathizers who might be persuaded to endorse his approach to suffering that pain can never be assuaged by religious platitudes that gloss over the truth about how it feels to be broken in two.

Job expects and hopes for something more from his friends—and from God. He is not closed to honest advice and sound instruction, but what he most needs is companionship, not so much to ease the pain but to improve the quality of suffering. In *A Whole New Life*, Reynolds Price offers personal reflections that speak to those who would comfort the Jobs of this world. He writes about his midlife war with the cancer that invaded his body and grew up his spine like an eel. He survived, although with a paralysis that bears witness to the battle, and from the "far side of catastrophe," what he calls "the dim other side of that high wall that effectively shuts disaster off from the unfazed world," he articulates the sufferer's need: "In that deep trough I needed companions more than prayers or potions that had worked for another."[93]

Too often what he received from those who wanted to care was something very different. Some of his friends provided "would-be helpful books" that explained why he had cancer—perhaps his own unhealthy habits?—how some new treatment might miraculously cure it—had he tried "moon-rock dust and beetle-wing ointment"?—and, as a last resort, what kind of deal he might cut with God to salvage any life he could—if I give You all the feeling in my legs, and all the control of my upper body, will You permit me a few extra years? His physicians, highly skilled professionals who were

93. R. Price, *A Whole New Life* (New York: Athenium, 1994), 180.

trained to treat cancer patients, sometimes offered little or no real comfort. His oncologist turned away from him when he attempted casual conversation in the halls. The doctor seemed unable to offer an unscripted word of encouragement or a spontaneous expression of comfort. Price's wonderment about such treatment places him in the company of Job:

> Did he [the doctor] think I was brewing my grievance against him, some costly revenge in the crowded market of malpractice suits? Did he shy from involvement with one more face that was hungry for life though already stamped *Dead?* My best guess from here is, he didn't know how to act otherwise; and he hadn't tried to learn. It's often said by way of excuse that doctors are insufficiently trained for humane relations. For complex long-range interaction with damaged creatures, they may well need a kind of training they never receive; but what I wanted and needed badly, from that man then, was the frank exchange of decent concern. When did such a basic transaction between two mammals require postgraduate instruction beyond our mother's breast?[94]

Perhaps there is no adequate training for long-range, complex companionship with "damaged creatures" like Job. It is true that offering real comfort and consolation to those who suffer is never easy and may be costly. The more intimate we become with those who hurt, the more their pain becomes our own. But Job would insist that when such comfort is lacking, everyone is diminished, not just the afflicted. People who do not or will not comfort those who suffer, whether because of fear or indifference, forsake the summons and the opportunity to image God by loving as God loves. The summons and what is at stake when we fail to heed it is not different in the New Testament:

> Beloved, let us love one another, because love is from God; everyone who loves is born of God and knows God. . . . Those who say, "I love God," and hate their brothers and sisters, are liars; for those who do not love a brother or a sister whom they have seen, cannot love God whom they have not seen. (1 John 4:7, 20)

---

94. Ibid., 56.

We return one more time to Carpaccio's painting. (See Figure 4.4, Carpaccio, *Meditation on the Passion of Christ.*) We look again at his depiction of Job. We see again Job's frail, withered body. We look again at the shattered skull with its empty eye sockets that can no longer see, the severed jaw that can no longer speak, the fractured leg bone that can no longer walk and run—all symbolic reminders of how much death Job experienced in life. We see again that he points to his feet, now covered with flimsy sandals, the only protection left to him for walking through a life full of too much pain. We remember the words he repeated so often to friends who could not or would not respond: "Please look at me; Please listen carefully to what I am saying about what it feels like to be me; Please look at me . . . and flinch." We remember the words that Jesus will speak to his disciples on the other side of death—"Look at my hands and feet . . . . Touch me and see"—and we wonder if Jesus has not learned these from Job.

We look again at Job, this time at his head, so weary he must hold it up with his hand. We see his eyes staring blankly at the horizon—in our direction—as if he is still looking for someone who may yet appear and hear what he is saying. We see the granite block on which he sits. And perhaps now, for the first time, we see that the block bears a Hebrew inscription. [FIGURE 4.7] The words are "My redeemer lives,"[95] which come from Job 19:25, perhaps the most famous sentence in the book that preserves his story: "I know that my Redeemer lives."[96] But the inscription, like the hope that it voices, is broken off. Like Job, it needs repairing. These words of broken hope beg a question: Who will be Job's redeemer?

The Hebrew word for "redeemer" is *gōʾēl*. The word comes from the field of family law. It designates the nearest male relative—brother, paternal uncle, cousin—who is duty-bound to protect and preserve the family when his kinsman is unable to do so. The responsibilities of the *gōʾēl* include buying back family property that has fallen into the hands of outsiders (Lev 25-28; Ruth 4:3-6), redeeming a relative sold into slavery (Lev 25:47-49), and marrying a widow to provide

---

95. P. Humfrey, *Carpaccio* (London: Chaucer Press, 2005), 119.

96. For discussion of the inscription, see F. Hartt, "Carpaccio's *Meditation on the Passion*," *Arts Bulletin* 22 (1940): 25–35.

FIGURE 4.7

Vittore Carpaccio. Detail of *Meditation on the Passion of Christ.*

an heir for her dead husband (as in the famous case of Ruth; see Ruth 3:12-13; 4:5). In religious usage, God is described as the *gōʾēl* of those who have fallen into distress or bondage (as, for example, those who are slaves in Egypt: Exod 6:6; 15:13; Ps 74:2). We may take special note of the affirmation that God acts as *gōʾēl,* "redeemer," for those who are too helpless or too vulnerable to fend for themselves (Ps 119:154; Prov 23:11; Jer 50:34; Lam 3:58).

So who is the redeemer Job looks for? If we stay focused on the Old Testament's story of Job, then we may suspect that Job hopes a family member might come to his aid. But the tragedy of his story is that his family is dead. We may expect that he hopes a friend will come to comfort and console him. But the credentials of his friends—Eliphaz, Bildad, and Zophar—hardly give him any reason to believe that they are willing to be his redeemer. We may expect that he longs for God to be his redeemer. But the book of Job causes us to wonder about this, because according to the text, Job searches in vain, through thirty-five chapters, for some assurance of God's presence. At every step along this painful journey, God is silent. From Job's perspective, it appears that his hopes for a redeemer are dashed, no matter where he looks, like this broken piece of inscription in Carpaccio's painting.

If we shift our thoughts to the New Testament, we may take some comfort in the promise of the resurrection, for we hold it true that Christ offers eternal life, even to those who have died in faith. Perhaps we may think of Job as the Old Testament's version of Jesus' parable about the rich man and Lazarus (Luke 16:19-31). Ignored and abandoned in life, the poor, sore-covered man named Lazarus (read Job), will be carried away in death, there to be comforted in the bosom of Abraham, until Jesus comes to make all things right. As a Christian, I affirm with you the promise of resurrection. Like you, I am brought to the edge of my seat when I hear the stirring words of the "Hallelujah Chorus" in Handel's *Messiah* (first performed in Dublin in 1742). When Handel responds to Job's words, "I know that my Redeemer liveth," by citing by Paul's words from 1 Corinthians, "Thanks be to God who gives us the victory through our Lord Jesus Christ" (1 Cor 15:57), I want to stand up and applaud.

But I want to press us to think carefully about what the promise of resurrection offers to the Jobs of the world. If in life the Jobs of the world are abandoned and ignored, if in life they yearn for a presence that does not come until they die, if they cry out for comfort in a world that seems oblivious to their pain, the hope of justice and redemption in death notwithstanding, is that what God wants? Is that what the Lenten journey requires of us? If we are content to leave the role of comforting the suffering to Jesus, confident that in his hands the final outcome is not really in doubt, then perhaps we need not bother too much with Luke's account of the Passion. Perhaps, when we hear Jesus say to those who claim to be his disciples, "Look at my hands and feet . . . . Touch me and see," we too may be content to feel nothing more than disbelief and wonder (Luke 24:41). But if Jesus really expects us to touch and feel what it means to be "grieved, even to death" (Matt 26:38), then perhaps this Lenten journey requires something more from us. I return to the question I posed at the end of the second presentation. When we stand before Jesus at the end of this journey and he asks us, "Do you have anything to eat?" (Luke 24:41), that is, do you have anything to feed people like me, people who have died with the unanswered question, "My God, my God, why have you forsaken me?" on their lips, what will we say? What will we offer that will make a difference in life, not only in death?

I leave you with these words from Tennyson, which give voice to the hope of the Jobs of the world who sit alone on the ash heap, hoping against hope that someone will hear, that someone will see and be appalled, that someone will flinch enough to come before it is too late:

> Come not, when I am dead,
> To drop thy foolish tears upon my grave,
> To trample round my fallen head,
> And vex the unhappy dust thou wouldst not save.
> There let the wind sweep and the plover cry;
> But thou go by.

5

"Let Love Clasp Grief Lest Both Be Drowned"

We have come to the fifth and last of these presentations. We have pondered the imperative in the Gospel of John's passion account, "Behold the man" (*Ecce Homo*; John 19:5). The words are spoken by Pilate, who instructs the crowd to look at Jesus, bound, scourged, crowned with thorns, and wearing a bloodstained purple robe. Pilate washes his hands of responsibility and hands this "man of sorrows" (Isa 53:3) over to the crowd to do with him as they wish. The Lenten journey invites us to take our place with that crowd who gathered long ago outside Pilate's headquarters. Like them, we are onlookers; like them, Pilate's imperative requires us to look at this Jesus and decide what we will do with him.

We have also been thinking about a second imperative, which comes to us from the resurrected Christ, who says, "Look at my hands and feet . . . . Touch me and see" (Luke 24:39). These words, spoken by one who knows firsthand what it means to suffer brokenness and loss, address us not as onlookers but as insiders. Indeed, the resurrected Christ speaks as if he counts us among his intimate disciples, as if we too are now invited to touch and feel the hands and feet that teach us what it means to be "deeply grieved, even to death" (Matt 26:38 and parallels).

At every step along this journey, both of these imperatives have been itching at our consciences, waiting for our response. These two imperatives—"Behold the man" and "Look at my hands and feet"—along with the questions that trail in their wake return us to the suggestion I began with in the first presentation. What are we supposed to *see* when we "*behold* the man"? What are we supposed to *feel* when the resurrected Christ says, "*Touch* me"? How we answer these questions, I believe, will determine in large measure where the Lenten journey has led us. The time for deciding how we will respond has come. We approach Palm Sunday, the time when we must decide whether we will follow Jesus into Jerusalem, where a cross is being prepared for him—and for us. The next Sunday is Easter, when we will stand before an empty tomb and decide whether our words and our deeds will do justice to what we have learned.

I. TAKING UP THE CROSS IN A POST-RESURRECTION WORLD

If we are to follow Jesus as he heads into Jerusalem, then we must think hard about some difficult instructions. Matthew reports that when Jesus set his sights on the journey to Jerusalem, he began to prepare his disciples for what would be required of them. He must go to Jerusalem, Jesus said, to "undergo great suffering . . . and be killed, and on the third day be raised" (Matt 16:22). When Peter heard this, he took hold of Jesus and rebuked him. "God forbid it, Lord! This must never happen to you." Jesus responded to Peter with a rebuke of his own, for Peter's notion of serving God by avoiding suffering was not Jesus' way. Jesus spelled out his way with chilling clarity: "If any want to become my followers, let them deny themselves and take up their cross and follow me. For those who want to save their life will lose it, and those who lose their life for my sake will find it" (Matt 16:24-25).

"If any want to become my followers, let them deny themselves and take up their cross and follow me." If any want to become my followers . . . . In the last presentation we looked at Piero della Francesca's painting of the resurrected Christ. (See Figure 2.5.) We focused on Christ's right foot, still in the grave, as if he had not yet fully stepped into the hope and promise of resurrection. We looked at his eyes, staring into the foreground, as if he was looking straight at us. (See Figure 2.6, detail of face.) We looked at those eyes, etched with the fresh memory of pain. We remembered Wallace Stegner's commentary on this painting—"Those who have been dead under-stand things that will never be understood by those who have only lived"—and we wondered, what does Jesus understand, and what does he want to teach us, about what it feels like to be dead? In his eulogy for William Butler Yeats (died January 1939), W. H. Auden wrote, "The words of a dead man / Are modified in the guts of the living."[97] How, we wonder, will the words of the once-dead, now-resurrected Christ be modified in us?

In the previous presentation, we imagined what Jesus might have learned when "he descended into hell," as the Apostles' Creed puts it, there to commune with the righteous souls who preceded him in death, like Job, as the artist Carpaccio so evocatively suggests. (See Figure 4.4, Carpaccio [1450–1525], *Meditation on the Passion of Christ.*) We listened in as Job told Jesus his story: how he had grieved the loss of his children, seven sons and three daughters, dead "for no reason" (Job 2:3); how he had yearned for the comforting assurance of the presence of God; how he discovered that his sole "comfort" was the glib counsel of misguided friends whose theology mandated that the fault was his. The price for a word from God, they insisted, was his admission that his children died because of his sin. We heard Job protest his innocence. We imagined him teaching Jesus that all the Jobs of the world hope for a redeemer, and we exegeted his hope with the plaintive words of Tennyson, "Come not when I am dead."

In this final presentation, we look again at della Francesca's painting, and this time I invite you to focus on Christ's left foot, the foot that is about to step into life on the other side of death. [FIGURE 5.1] We look because the Lenten journey we make as followers of Christ does not summon us to stay at the cross, where death seems to be the final word, but to go forward into life, where the Word must become flesh and blood. In real life, the Word become flesh and blood can be bruised and broken. In this real world, we keep stumbling upon one Job after another, each one sitting on his or her own ash heap of suffering "for no reason," each one hoping against hope for someone who will offer comfort *before*, not *after*, they die. The question before us as we head into Holy Week is, who will be

---

97. W. H. Auden, "In Memory of W. B. Yeats," *W. H. Auden Collected Poems,* ed. E. Mendelson (New York: Vintage International, 1991), 247.

FIGURE 5.1

Piero della Francesca (1415–1492). *The Resurrection*. c. 1462–1464. Mural
in fresco and tempera. Museo Civico di Sansepolcro. (Credit: Wikimedia
Commons, PD–US)

the redeemer of these Jobs? If we commit ourselves to follow the
resurrected Christ not only into death *but also* into life wisened by
death, what will we offer to the broken and bruised of this world,
who desperately need someone to make a difference in their lives?

Imagine, if you will, the post-resurrection world into which
della Francesca's Jesus leads us. Having grieved with Jesus "even unto
death," having touched and felt the hands and feet of One who can
teach us more than anyone who has only lived, where do we who

profess to be his disciples go from here? The question is freighted and far from simple, for the world that lies before us seems at once both deeply needful of comfort and overwhelmingly impervious to any facile consolation that only pretends to make a difference.

The statistics and the images that give definition to this post-resurrection world of suffering into which Jesus steps, the world in which we would be his disciples, are more than cause for pause. It is estimated that from 1915 to 1945 (i.e., from the start of World War I to the end of World War II) some seventy million, including six million Jews in Nazi Germany, died in Europe and Russia as the result of various acts of human barbarism. It is a period so defined by the horrors of death, destruction, and inhumanity that G. Steiner has described it as a "season in hell."[98] The word "*season*" may be too optimistic, for it suggests that this hell on earth has an ending point that can be placed on the calendar. Like the seasons of the year, the coldness and death of winter, we may trust, will one day be replaced by spring, when life will once again be the measure of our days. But the facts do not support the hope. 1945 has come and gone. We stopped Hitler, but the genocide he orchestrated seems to go on and on, and the numbers keep adding up: Pakistan slaughtered three million Bengalis; Nigeria exterminated two to three million Ibos; the Indonesians slaughtered between 60,000 and 100,000 in East Timor; Idi Amin murdered some 500,000 fellow Ugandans; the Tutsis massacred 100,000–200,000 Hutus in Burundi; the Sudanese murdered 500,000 in the south of Sudan; and I've not even factored in the French torture of Algerians, Pol Pot's cruelties in Cambodia, the Bosnian war, or the suffering that we read about in today's head-lines in Palestine, Iraq, and Iran. When we look on our world as persons of faith, even on this side of resurrection, it is hard to deny the unsettling truth of the Jewish theologian Arthur Cohen. The "*sovereignty of evil*," he asserts, has "become more real and immediate and familiar than [the *sovereignty of*] *God*."[99] The sheer numbers of the Jobs and the ash heaps strewn across this world seem to reduce

---

98. G. Steiner, *In Bluebeard's Castle: Some Notes on the Redefinition of Culture* (New Haven: Yale University Press, 1971), 29–56.

99. A. Cohen, *The Tremendum: A Theological Interpretation of the Holocaust* (New York: Crossroad, 1988), 34 (emphasis added).

all our celebrations of God's "very good" creation (Gen 1:31) to little more than sacramental nonsense.

The journey we have made may be visualized by contrasting two different artistic images of humanity, both of which seek to exemplify what God meant when deciding to create human beings in the divine image. [FIGURE 5.2] The first is Michelangelo's magnificent Renaissance statue of David (1501–1504), located in the Galleria dell'Accademia in Florence. Michelangelo wanted to capture the strength, courage, and confidence of the young David as he was preparing to go into battle with the Philistine giant, Goliath (1 Sam 17:1-58). We see the laser-focused pupils in David's eyes, the deep curls in his hair, the flexing thigh muscles in his right leg, the pulsing veins on the back of his left hand. If we look closely, we can see the slingshot in the left hand, the rock cupped in the right hand. But in truth, these details are only secondary. What commands our attention is the towering body, so strong, so anatomically perfect; the head, turned resolutely toward the challenge; the eyes, fixed on a victory that is never in doubt. The statue is so evocative of the best and brightest of God's hopes and expectations for human beings that we have little difficulty in understanding why the city of Florence adopted it as its symbol. They saw in it the promise of victory against whatever challenges and obstacles might come their way. Michelangelo was twenty-six years old when he began work on *David*. Some thirty years later he rendered another, less assured, vision of humanity in the four unfinished nude male statues now located in the Galleria's Hall of Prisoners, within sight of *David*. Each of the statues depicts a man, variously identified as "slave," "prisoner," or "captive," who has not yet fully emerged out of the marble. The representation is emblematic of "the eternal struggle of human beings to free themselves from their material trappings." The fourth statue, *Prisoner or Captive Known as Atlas*, is of a man carrying a huge weight that seems to compress his head, barely visible, into his body.[100] [FIGURE 5.3] Neither anatomically perfect nor heroically confident, the fate of this man, like the primordial Titan who was condemned to bear the weight of the heavens on his shoulders, is anything but certain.

---

100. For a brief description of "The Atlas," see the Galleria dell'Accademia website: accademia.org/explore-museum/artworks/michelangelos-prisoners-slaves.

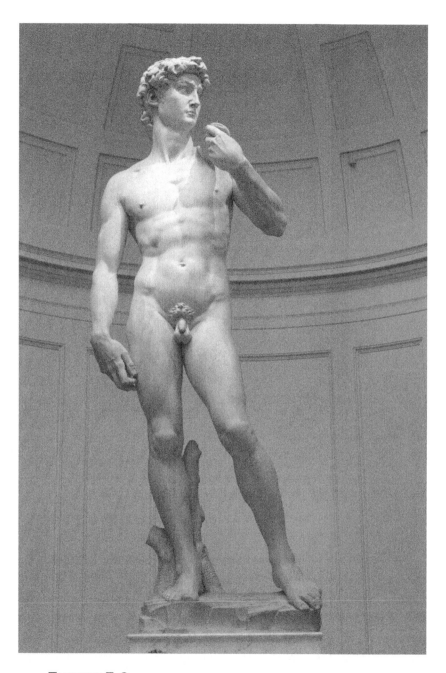

FIGURE 5.2

Michelangelo. *David*. 1501–1504. Marble. Galleria dell'Accademia, Florence. (Credit: Wikipedia Commons, CCA 3.0)

FIGURE 5.3

Michelangelo. *Prisoner or Captive Known as Atlas.* c. 1530–1534. For
the tomb of Pope Julius II (1443–1513). Unfinished marble sculpture.
Galleria dell'Academia, Florence, Italy. (Credit: Wikimedia Commons,
CCA–SA4.0)

A second visual, the Mauthausen Memorial in the Pére Lachaise
Cemetery in Paris, which is modeled after "The Atlas," is more
explicit. [FIGURE 5.4] The artist, Gérard Choain, was a prisoner
of war in 1939–1945. He sculpted a bronze figure, representative of
prisoners in the German concentration camp in Mauthausen, Austria,
who were forced to carry blocks weighing fifty or more pounds while
climbing the 186 steps known as the "Stairs of Death." This emaciated prisoner balances the block on his shoulders with his right hand.
Its weight forces his head down; the veins in his neck bulge under
the pressure. With his left hand he steadies himself; knees bent, he

FIGURE 5.4

Gérard Choain. Mauthausen Concentration Camp Memorial at Pére
Lachaise Cemetery, Paris. Dedicated May 4, 1958. (Credit: Wikimedia
Commons, CCA–SA4.0)

stagger-steps his way towards the unseen top of the quarry. From the
Renaissance to the death camps. From hope to despair. From heroic,
god-like aspiration to imprisoned, pointless existence. How did we
go from this (Michelangelo's *David*) to this (Michelangelo's *Atlas*) to
this (Choain's emaciated prisoner depicted on the memorial)?

"If any want to become to become my followers, let them deny
themselves and take up their cross and follow me." How are we to
follow Jesus into a world like this? There is so much suffering; where
do we begin? There is so much suffering; what can we possibly do that
will make a difference? It is little wonder that almost any response we

consider leaves us stewing in a mix of unclear emotional responses. Every time we think we are getting enough traction to move forward, we find ourselves miring up again up in the muck and mud of indecision lacquered with a queasy indifference. Consider, for example, two possible responses from opposite ends of the spectrum.

(1) Thomas Lynch is a contemporary funeral director and armchair theologian who lives in Milford, Michigan. He has been described as a cross between the humorist Garrison Keillor and the poet William Butler Yeats. He has written award-winning poetry and fiction, which speaks of what he has observed about how we respond to death and dying in this modern age. In a book of essays titled *Bodies in Motion and at Rest*, he notes that cable television, print media, and the internet have given us all instant access to the atrocities that occur in this world. If something horrendous happens on the other side of the world, pictures, print, and commentary will be on our cell phones or "smart" watches in a matter of minutes. We are hard wired into the grief of this world, whether we wish to be or not.

The *upside* of this instant access to the pain and grief of others is that information from all over the world is at our fingertips. We can no longer hide behind the claims of innocence or ignorance. "We did not know" is no longer an adequate response to the afflicted in this world. The *downside* of being constantly flooded by images of suffering from around the world, what Lynch refers to as the steady diet of "tragedy-cam" and "Grief TV," is that we become numb from overexposure. Looking on pain and suffering becomes a spectator sport. We watch as long as the "game" holds our interest, but when the outcome seems no longer in doubt, we simply change the channel in search of more entertainment. He makes the point as follows:

> Tragedy-cam and Grief TV give couch potatoes easy access to the "therapies" of "national mourning" for people they have no acquaintance with or knowledge of or interest in except as covers on the magazines in waiting rooms and checkout lines. With round-the-clock coverage on three cable channels and network news magazines and special reports, no one need change their schedule, put on a suit, order flowers, bake a casserole, go to the funeral home or church, try to find something of comfort to say or endure the difficult quiet of genuine grief when words fail, when

nothing can be said. Nor need they see a body or help carry one or pay for anything, or perpetually care. They needn't budge. The catharsis is user-friendly, the "healing" home delivered. "Being there" for perfect strangers has never been easier. When they've had enough they can grab a Dove Bar, flick to The Movie Channel or the Home Shopping Network and wait until the helicopters locate another outrage to zoom in on.[101]

Whatever we "couch potatoes" experience when we channel surf through the miseries of this world, Lynch says, "it is not grief."

> Grief is the tax we pay on our attachments, not on our interests or diversions or entertainments. *We grieve in keeping with the table stakes of our relationships, according to the emotional capital we invest in the lives and times of others,* that portion of ourselves we ante up before the cards are dealt. We might be curious about our losses when we play to kill time, or interested when we play for fun, or even obsessed a little if we find the game compelling. But we grieve for losses only in games we play for keeps—real love, real hate, real attachments broken.[102]

(2) A second possible response comes from the other end of the spectrum. Because there are so many instances in history of inexplicable suffering, there is a temptation to isolate one as *the example* that defines all others; *one exemplar,* under which all other cases may be subsumed. I suspect the case that comes first to mind for most of us is the historic suffering of the Jews during World War II, a period now conveyed in the streamlined and highly emotive term, *the Holocaust* (note the singularizing function of the article "the").

On this point, I am struck by the observations of the Jewish writer Phillip Lopate. In his last collection of essays, Lopate includes a piece he titles "Resistance to the Holocaust."[103] He begins anecdotally, with a memory from his childhood. He recalls how, in the

---

101. T. Lynch, *Bodies in Motion and at Rest: On Metaphor and Mortality* (New York: Norton, 2000), 193–94.

102. Ibid., 194 (emphasis added).

103. P. Lopate, "Resistance to the Holocaust," in *Getting Personal: Selected Writings* (New York: Basic Books, 2003), 263–79.

years just after World War II had ended, his mother dragged him around Brooklyn to visit some of the newly arrived Jewish refugees from Europe. He would sit for hours in somebody's kitchen while his mother talked with these women, usually in Yiddish, a strange, seemingly secretive language Phillip didn't understand, about what it had been like in Nazi Germany. After they left, his mother would say to him in a hushed voice, "Did you see the number on her arm? She was in a concentration camp." Lopate says he did not understand why his mother was so fixated on these victims or why she wanted him to share her preoccupation with them. It seemed like his mother was trying to warn him that "*the* Holocaust" was some kind of rhetorical "bully," poised to rough him up if he did not kowtow to its demands for "compassionate awe." For reasons not clear to him as a young boy, he resisted.

As he matured into Jewish adulthood, his resistance stiffened. The term "the Holocaust" seemed to be so rigidly exclusive. It was as if the addition of the definite article "the" rendered the Jewish experience of suffering unique, as if it was in a class by itself and therefore must not be mixed up or diluted by comparing it with other historical experiences of suffering. Lopate understood that what happened to the Jews in Nazi Germany has a special claim on our moral conscience for any number of reasons, including the following: (1) the *scale*—six million Jews—represents the largest number of deaths extracted from one single group; (2) the *technology*—the mechanization of the death factories—is unprecedented in history; (3) the *bureaucracy*—the involvement of the state apparatus—was used in ways previously unimagined; and (4) the *blatant intent*—to annihilate every last member of the Jewish people—that we want to believe is the absolute nadir of human bestiality.

Even so, Lopate worries that singling out "the Holocaust" freezes the horrors of this particular experience of suffering in history, as if nothing like it can or will ever happen again. Does this not invite us to assume, all too glibly, that "the Holocaust" was an aberration, a one-time fluke of human barbarity that will never be repeated? *If* "the Holocaust" is unique, then we need not be on guard against it happening again. But *if it is not unique*—and by any definition of pain and suffering, the statistics documenting the carnage of

post-Holocaust genocide around the globe confirm that *it is not*—
then how long can we afford to be smugly indifferent to the growing
numbers of Jobs in this world, who continue to die on their ash
heaps, still waiting for someone to take them seriously?

"If any want to become my followers, let them deny themselves
and take up their cross and follow me." Thus far, I have suggested
that the world in which we are summoned to follow Jesus offers us
two options. Given the massive number of Jobs in this world and
the constant technological intrusion of their cries into our settled
existence, we may yield to the temptation to become couch potatoes when it comes to identifying with their claim on our lives, as
Thomas Lynch suggests. Someone else has been brutalized in some
remote corner of the world. Another day, another victim bites the
dust. Ho-hum. We look, we flinch for a moment, then we change the
channel. Or, as Phillip Lopate suggests, we may fixate on one subset
of victims—in his case, the Jews—and on one unique and presumed
unrepeatable historical moment, when the norm for human compassion was temporarily displaced by an aberrant bestiality. Both
responses, I suggest, are inadequate for the imperatives of the Lenten
journey we are making. If we choose the first response, we become
in effect merely channel surfers in the world of grief; we look as long
as we are entertained, and then we push the remote-control button
and move on. If we choose the second response, then we hone in on
one particular example of human suffering to the exclusion of all
others, confident that being followers of Christ requires little more
of us than to become students of history's anomalies. Either way, we
remain passive onlookers to the pain and suffering of others. In the
meantime, Annie Dillard would remind us that "Christ hangs, as it
were," with all innocent victims of injustice, "on the cross forever,
always incarnate, and always nailed."[104]

II. WHO IS TO BLAME?

How are we to follow Jesus into a world like this? Jesus himself
models a third option that requires we move beyond the two we have
considered thus far. The Gospel of John records the story this way:

---

104. A. Dillard, *For the Time Being* (New York: Alfred A. Knopf, 1999), 169.

As Jesus walked along, he saw a man blind from birth. His disciples asked him, "Rabbi, who sinned, this man or his parents, that he was born blind?" Jesus answered, "Neither this man nor his parents sinned; he was born blind so that God's works may be revealed in him. We must work the works of him who sent me while it is day; night is coming when no one can work. As long as I am in world, I am the light of the world." When he had said this, he spat on the ground and made mud with his saliva and spread the mud on the man's eyes, saying to him, "Go wash in the pool of Siloam" (which means Sent). Then he went off and washed, and he came back able to see. (John 9:1-7)

The story is one of many in the Gospels that confirm Jesus healed the blind (cf. Matt 9:27-31; 20:29-34; Mark 8:22-26; 10:46-52; Luke 18:35-42). John's account shares elements with many of these other stories, but he adds a new twist that makes this story particularly relevant for our reflections here. As the disciples walked along with Jesus, presumably on their way to Jerusalem, they encountered a man who had been blind since birth. The disciples are the first to respond to the situation, and so we may be encouraged to think they will model for us a way of following Jesus toward Jerusalem that we should image. When we listen carefully to the story, however, we find that they still have much to learn about what it means to see, touch, feel, and make a difference in the lives of those who are afflicted.

They immediately look past this man, past his need for healing, to the theological problem he presents. "Rabbi, who sinned, this man or his parents?" Their question places them in the company of Job's friends, those who patronize the reality of suffering by turning it into an abstract problem to be solved from a distance. Like Job's friends, they assume that suffering is caused by sin. Like Job's friends, they assume that their responsibility is to find who is to blame, to wrench from them a confession of guilt, and then to fix the problem by exacting from the guilty party the appropriate penalty. As the cliché goes, "When in doubt, fix blame." The disciples never once speak to the blind man. They never once get close enough to understand what it feels like to be him, what it means to go through life without being able to see.

Jesus listens patiently to their question, then turns the conversation around. When encountering someone in need, the first response should not be to fix blame. "Neither this man nor his parents sinned," Jesus says. He was blind from birth; his affliction was not caused by anything he or his parents did. In other words, suffering is not a moral statement about someone's behavior or character. It is not a *problem* that requires us to do theology. It is not an *issue* that requires we stake out a position, a stance, on the meaning of suffering in this world. When we encounter someone in need, Jesus says, it is an opportunity, indeed a mandate, to show compassion. So it is that when Jesus looks on the blind man, he does not see a sinner. He sees an imperative to touch this man. Jesus says that blindness, or any other affliction that robs people of being the persons God intended them to be, is a chance for us to be about God's business. As Jesus puts it, the pain and suffering of others requires that Jesus' disciples let the work of God be done through them. "We must work the works of him who sent [us]," Jesus says, while there is time. The day will come when the needy are dead and the opportunity to reach out to them in compassion will be lost. So Jesus takes the spit from his own mouth, mixes it with the dirt from which all human beings come, and makes a healing ointment that he places on the blind eyes of the man. In sum, he reaches out and touches the man who needs help with his own life, and when he connects his life to the life of the needy, a miracle occurs: the man who once was blind can now see! [FIGURE 5.5]

III. JESUS' ETHIC OF LOVE

If we are to get our bearings on what is required of Jesus' disciples in *this world* of so much pain and suffering, perhaps we should ponder for a moment what our accountability will be in the *next world*. We return one last time to Piero della Francesca's depiction of Jesus, one foot in the grave, the other prepared to step into life eternal once God gives the word. (See Figure 5.1, della Francesca, *The Resurrection*, full view.) Can we imagine ourselves in this in-between position, between the reality of the life we lived in this world and our hope of the life to come in the next? What will we hear God say to us? What

FIGURE 5.5

El Greco depicts Jesus healing the blind man in the midst
of a crowd of onlookers. To the left, neighbors look toward
surrounding buildings trying to determine where the blind
man came from. In the foreground, the blind man's parents
appear to be en route to the scene, perhaps to confirm their
son had been blind since birth. To the right an agitated
group (Pharisees?) appears to be rebuking Jesus for healing
on the Sabbath. Apart from the blind parents, no one looks
directly at the man in need of healing. Other than Jesus, no
one reaches out to touch him.

El Greco. *Christ Healing the Blind Man.* c. 1570. Oil on canvas. Metropolitan Museum of Art, New York. (Credit: Gift of Mr. and Mrs. Charles
Wrightsman, 1978)

criteria will God use to decide whether we are worthy to step into the
life everlasting, the promise of resurrection?

Of the Gospel writers, only Matthew gives us any details of the
last judgment. Following a long series of six parables about what it
means to live responsibly so as to be ready for the coming of the Son

of Man (Matt 24:32–25:30), Matthew invites us to consider this scene:

> When the Son of Man comes in his glory, and all the angels with him, he will sit on the throne of his glory. All the nations will be gathered before him, and he will separate people from one another as a shepherd separates the sheep from the goats, and he will put the sheep at his right hand and the goats at the left. Then the king will say to those at his right hand, "Come, you that are blessed by my Father, inherit the kingdom prepared for you from the foundation of the world; for I was hungry and you gave me food, I was thirsty and you gave me something to drink, I was a stranger and you welcomed me, I was naked and you gave me clothing, I was sick and you took care of me, I was in prison and you visited me." Then the righteous will answer him, "Lord, when was it that we saw you hungry and gave you food, or thirsty and gave you something to drink? And when was it that we saw you a stranger and welcomed you, or naked and gave you clothing? And when was it that we saw you sick or in prison and visited you?" And the king will answer them, "Truly I tell you, just as you did it to the least of these who are members of my family, you did it to me."
>
> Then he will say to those at his left hand, "You that are accursed, depart from me into the eternal fire prepared for the devil and his angels; for I was hungry and you gave me no food, I was thirsty and you gave me nothing to drink, I was a stranger and you did not welcome me, naked and you did not give me clothing, sick and in prison and you did not visit me." Then they also will answer, "Lord, when was it that we saw you hungry or thirsty or a stranger or naked or sick or in prison, and did not take care of you?" Then he will answer them, "Truly I tell you, just as you did not do it to one of the least of these, you did not do it to me." And these will go away into eternal punishment, but the righteous into eternal life. (Matt 25:31-46)

According to Matthew, the single criterion for entry into eternal life is *not* confession of faith in Christ. Matthew says nothing of grace, justification, or the forgiveness of sin. He says nothing about our enthusiasm for singing Handel's "Hallelujah Chorus." Whether we join our voices to the choir and sing, "Hallelujah, Christ is risen; He is risen indeed," seems not to matter one whit. When we stand before God on the day of judgment, the only thing that matters is whether we have acted with loving care for needy people. To have seen them, touched them, and reached out to them with compassion that makes a difference is not a matter of earning "extra credit" with God, as if we can make up for something after death that we did not do in this life. According to Matthew, the one and only decisive criterion for entering the kingdom of God is doing *deeds* of love and mercy that feed the hungry, give drink to the thirsty, clothe the naked, and offer community and communion to strangers who have no place to call home. Addressing the post-resurrection community now charged with the responsibility of living in accordance with Jesus' model, the author of 1 John puts it this way:

> Beloved, let us love one another, because love is from God; everyone who loves is born of God and knows God. Whoever does not love does not know God, for God is love. . . . Those who say, "I love God," and hate their brothers and sisters are liars; for those who do not love a brother or a sister whom they have seen, cannot love God whom they have not seen. The commandment we have from him is this: those who love God must love their brothers and sisters also. (1 John 4:7-9, 20-21)

IV. "LET LOVE CLASP GRIEF LEST BOTH BE DROWNED"

"If any want to become my followers, let them deny themselves and take up their cross and follow me." If we are to take up the cross that has our name on it and follow Jesus into this world of too much pain and suffering, perhaps we should return once more to the foot of the cross, there to linger until we can learn what Jesus would teach us about the journey ahead. Toward this end, I invite you to reflect one last time on the difference between looking on someone else's pain as an insider or as an outsider.

Francisco de Goya invites us to reflect on the sufferings of Spanish citizens during their war with France in 1808.[105] (See Figure 3.1,

---

105. See the discussion above, pp. 61–63.

Francisco de Goya, "Not This!")In the picture, he shows three dead men hanging from trees, suggestively evocative of the three crosses on Golgotha. He focuses our attention on a dead man hanging limp from one of these trees and on one of Napoleon's soldiers who leans against a rock, looking at the scene from a distance. The literal space between the two is small, but the frame freezes the action, forcing us to consider the wordless, actionless proximity that seems to separate the two figures, perhaps forever. The weight of the dead man tilts the tree toward the soldier, but it has not yet made contact. The soldier's right foot is extended in the direction of the dead body ever so slightly, as if he may be about to rise up, reach out, and touch the corpse of the man who once was alive but now is dead. But in this frame, the French soldier is still sitting and looking on, perhaps thinking about what he should do. In any case, even if he should reach out, what good will it do? The man is already dead; the time for coming to his aid has already passed. So he and we sit and look and think about what might have been, if only he had reached out while there was still time to make a difference. De Goya makes no secret of what he thinks about those who, like this French soldier, are content to look on the suffering of others from a distance. His caption for this painting reads, "Not this!"

The second image is from Emile Nolde, whose painting of Christ's "Entombment" (1915) shows a very different picture. [FIGURE 5.6] Nolde captures the moment just after the dead Jesus has been lowered from the cross. To the left, a white bearded elderly man, perhaps Joseph of Arimathea, looks on with wide-eyed intensity as he wraps his arms around the feet of Jesus. To the right of Joseph, another face can be seen in the background, perhaps that of the beloved disciple John, whom the Gospels always depict as staying particularly close to Jesus. We see also his hand, which is wrapped around the nail-scarred hand of his beloved friend and master. To the far right is Mary, the mother of Jesus. She sits awkwardly, with her feet scrunched up under her body. Her lap provides a resting place for the body of her dead son. She wraps her arms around his neck, as if she is trying to pull Jesus back into the safety of her womb. Her posture suggests her fear that if she lets go, her son will slip from her grasp forever. Her head is buried behind his, so that *his* face, darkened

FIGURE 5.6

Emile Nolde. *The Entombment*. 1915. Oil on canvas. National Museum of Art, Architecture and Design, Oslo, Norway. (Credit: Wikipedia.org, PD-pre-1925 non-US)

by death, seems now to be *her* face. Each of these three figures makes physical contact with Jesus. Indeed, they each are so close to him that together their bodies form a U-shaped cradle, which surrounds the Jesus they loved and lost with a tactile compassion that brooks no space between them.[106]

Nolde's depiction of the grief and loss felt by these three who cradle Jesus' dead body calls to mind the words of Alfred Lord Tennyson's (1809–1892) poem "In Memoriam A. H. H." He describes the loss he experienced upon the sudden and tragic death of his best friend Arthur Hallam on September 15, 1833, at the age of twenty-two. Hallam had befriended Tennyson at Cambridge. He

---

106. For discussion of the painting, see Dillenberger, *Style and Content in Christian Art*, 201–206; cf. P. Selz, *Emile Nolde* (Museum of Modern Art, New York in collaboration with the San Francisco Museum of Art and the Pasadena Art Museum; Garden City, New York: Doubleday, 1963), 24.

had introduced Tennyson to the undergraduate literary group, the Apostles, helped him with his first publications of poetry, traveled with him to the Pyrenees and the Rhineland, and counseled him through difficult periods of loneliness and despair. At the time of his death, Hallam was engaged to marry Tennyson's sister, Emily. They were best friends, brothers in the deepest sense of the word. When Tennyson learned of Hallam's death, he began almost immediately to compose the words of this poem. They had shared a friendship for but five years. He worked on this poem, trying to find the words that matched what he had lost, for sixteen years. His hope, as he put it in the line that I have used for the title of this presentation, was to "Let love clasp Grief lest both be drown'd."[107] His lyrics make his loss of Hallam's friendship almost palpable. They are not Scripture, but they may be sacred nonetheless:

> One writes that "other friends remain,"
> > That "loss is common to the race" —
> > And common is the commonplace,
> And vacant chaff well meant for grain.
>
> That loss is common would not make
> > My own loss less bitter, rather more.
> > Too common! Never morning wore
> To evening, but some heart did break . . . . (6.1–8)
>
> I know that this was Life, — the track
> > Whereon with equal feet we fared;
> > And then, as now, the day prepared
> The daily burden for the back.
>
> But this it was that made me move
> > As light as carrier-birds in air;
> > *I loved the weight I had to bear,*
> *Because it needed help of Love;*
>
> Nor could I weary, heart or limb,
> > When mighty love would cleave in twain
> > The lading of a single pain,

---

107. Alfred Lord Tennyson, "In Memoriam A. H. H." in *Tennyson's Poetry*, selected and edited by R. Hill (New York, London: W. W. Norton, 1971), 1.10, p. 121.

And part it, giving half to him. (25.1–12; emphasis added)

And then these words, written during the holidays of the first Christmas after Hallam's death, which I trust you will recognize:

I hold it true, whate'er befall;
    I feel it, when I sorrow most;
'T is better to have loved and lost
Than never to have loved at all. (27.13–16)

"Let love clasp grief, lest both be drowned." What if this were the lesson Jesus wanted his disciples to learn on that day long ago when he said to them, "Look at my hands and feet . . . . Touch me and see"? How would the world be different if we were to take this as our "great commission"? What if on this side of the cross and the resurrection, on the other side of Easter, we became convicted that to follow Jesus means that we must go out into this world and let love clasp grief wherever we may find it? What might it mean to cradle the suffering ones of this world in a love that will not let go, no matter what?

If we are not only to *look* at the hands and feet of those whose lives have left them bruised and broken but also to *touch* them and *feel* their pain, then our Sunday morning Easter rituals will not be enough. Somehow we must alleviate the pain that gnaws at their bodies and numbs their souls. Somehow love must hold on to grief, lest both be drowned in a sea of unassuaged misery that threatens to reduce every "Hallelujah, Christ is risen" to sacramental babble.

As we lean into the final stages of this journey with Christ toward Jerusalem and Emmaus, I leave you with the two imperatives with which we began. "Behold the man!" And from this man who knows firsthand what it means to be "deeply grieved, even to death," this second imperative: "Look at my hands and feet . . . . Touch me and see." Once we touch and see what it feels like to be wounded, neither our confessions of faith nor the acts of mercy and compassion that incarnate them should ever be same again.

List of Figures

Figure 4.5   William Blake (1757–1827). *Book of Job*. Plate 7: "Job's Comforters," from *Illustrations of the Book of Job*. 1825–1826. Engraving. Metropolitan Museum of Art, New York, NY. (Credit: Gift of Edward Berment, 1917)

Figure 4.6   William Blake (1757–1827). *Book of Job*. Plate 10: "Job Rebuked by His Friends," from *Illustrations of the Book of Job*. 1825–1826. Engraving. Metropolitan Museum of Art, New York, NY. (Credit: Gift of Edward Berment, 1917)

Figure 4.7   Vittore Carpaccio. Detail of *Meditation on the Passion of Christ*.

Figure 5.1   Piero della Francesca (1415–1492). *The Resurrection*. c. 1462–1464. Mural in fresco and tempera. Museo Civico di Sansepolcro. (Credit: Wikimedia Commons, PD-US)

Figure 5.2   Michelangelo. *David*. 1501–1504. Marble. Galleria dell'Accademia, Florence. (Credit: Wikipedia Commons, CCA 3.0)

Figure 5.3   Michelangelo. *Prisoner or Captive Known as Atlas*. c. 1530–1534. For the tomb of Pope Julius II (1443–1513). Unfinished marble sculpture. Galleria dell'Accademia, Florence, Italy. (Credit: Wikimedia Commons, CCA-SA 4.0)

Figure 5.4   Gérard Choain. Mauthausen Concentration Camp Memorial at Pére Lachaise Cemetery, Paris. Dedicated May 4, 1958. (Credit: Wikimedia Commons, CCA-SA 4.0)

Figure 5.5   El Greco. *Christ Healing the Blind Man*." c. 1570. Oil on canvas. Metropolitan Museum of Art, New York. (Credit: Gift of Mr. And Mrs. Charles Wrightsman, 1978)

Figure 5.6   Emile Nolde. *The Entombment*. 1915. Oil on canvas. National Museum of Art, Architecture and Design, Oslo, Norway. (Credit: Wikipedia.org, PD-pre-1925 non-US)